ITCH

PANDEMIC POEMS

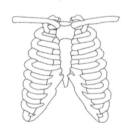

ITCH

PANDEMIC POEMS

• July 2020-April 21 •

Josie Lynn Richards

*For Jeremiah,
who is extraordinary*

Foreword

Itch, Josie Richards' memoir in poetry, takes a sensitive look at the emotional toll of the COVID-19 pandemic. The speaker of these pictures of everyday life is honest and observant, totally willing to share her own sensibility and lived experiences. In speaking of the sudden quietness of life in *Highly Sensitive Person on Hold,* she says, *Not every empty space / has to be filled with noise! / scents! / lights! / additives! / spice!* and concludes by saying, *our souls need rest.*

Yet, despite her contentment at home, Richards is aware of the struggles and personal difficulties other people are suffering. *Old Folks Home* memorializes a scene so many people have experienced as institutions and families try to cope with death and dying. As Richards says, *We mourn / and do our best / standing outside of their windows / on our fancy phones / trying to nudge / a smile.*

This writer is a close observer of all that crosses her path. The animals and insects are *simply & delicately [going] about their creaturely business (Don't Mind Me).* A local groundhog she calls Gertrude runs for cover when she senses a dog nearby, but what makes the poem memorable is Richards' imagined future when Gertrude will eat *clover / dandelions / raspberries / grubs / in the hot sun / again.* Surely we all long for summer, but knowing we share the pleasure of sun and ripe raspberries with a fellow creature makes that longing more poignant (*Gertrude Groundhog*).

Finally, even in the midst of a pandemic, Richards' poems are lovely reminders that the human heart doesn't stop because of isolation orders or fears of infection. She writes, *Somebody sits on your heart / like a song that you can't get out of your head. / You carry him around all day, like a teething child / like a toothache, the Holy Spirit pressing upon you / like a shadow with teeth (not breaking the skin.)* (*Somebody*). The collection touches on a range of human emotions. Here are people who miss their loved ones, and need their day jobs, and yet find solace in nature and in solitude, whether it's voluntary or enforced.

Dawn McDuffie

"A year of earth-grief and of bitter news"

-May Sarton, "Small Joys," *Coming Into Eighty*

...

"Help. Enter this mess."

"In the face of everything, we slowly come through."

-Anne Lamott, *Help Thanks Wow:*
The Three Essential Prayers

...

"Hope is a strategy during hard times, man."

-Dave Hollis

"Search me, O God, and know my heart;
Try me, and know my anxieties;
And see if there is any wicked way in me,
And lead me in the way everlasting."

-Psalm 139.23, 24 (NKJV)

For the Socially Anxious Souls

For the socially anxious souls among us,
this whole staying in
and keeping one's distance from people
and disguising oneself in public by wearing a face mask
& signature dark sunglasses
is, dare we say—
because *obviously* we don't wish for all of this sadness
and madness & weirdness—
a happy development.

Life these days is complicated & disordered
and hard to bear, to be sure,
but easier, to be oneself, in a sense,
for the socially anxious (& agoraphobic) soul.

Staying home has always been best.

And, after being in public, around people, with people—
safely and quite comfortably distanced—
because avoiding people is caring!—
one's energy hasn't been
completely depleted!

07.27.20

Puttering & Poetry/This Little Piggy Stayed Home

I rather like this new life
of working less
and keeping to the home,
the putting off of nonessential things
till tomorrow,
of puttering & poetry.

I rather like this new life
of being rewarded with a blue ribbon
for staying hemmed in,
the pressure to socialize
and to go places, gone out the window,
so to speak.

I rather like this new life
of interiors & mirrors,
of spending time alone
and with my people,
even though
my piggy bank
is panicking.

...

And I do realize
that I'm privileged (not like
living-in-a-mansion-driving-a-Lexus privileged),
aware that some people
are down to
their last pennies:

From where will the money come
for rent, gas,
for milk and bread,
period products
& & Kleenex®?

08.10.20

On Pandemic Time

I BRAKE FOR YOGA PANTS

-bumper sticker

We have lost a lot *a lot* during this pandemic
but we have gained, too.

A blessing in disguise during this time
has been time.

...

Even now, when we are swimming in time,
the days are remarkably short:
Where has the day up & gone?

If you're like me, I'm Greedy for time.
There is, alas, never enough
time to do all that I want to do in a day.

I don't know how in the world people find time
for yoga, or reading, or knitting, or prayer.

...

This is how: They make time.

They rise an hour before their children wake,
or forgo watching another episode of blank,
or they steal away time
whenever & wherever they can find it.

Still, for others; parents of hungry children,
or adult children caring for languishing parents,
time stretches on into infinity—
they count down the hours
till the stars shine & a glass of wine (or, water)
is, at last, acceptable (or, attainable).

*

Whatever your feelings about time,
in whatever season or circumstance you find yourself,
the silky blue river runs on with or without you.

It's up to you to decide how to spend
your gracious measure of time,
remembering that our days
are short sticks.

And, also, our days
are long legs
with which to go and do
whatever it is you have always dreamed of doing.

Amen & Amen.

07.28.20

The Highly Sensitive Person On Hold

Can we just agree
to stop the static,
the elevator music,
the recorded message,
the beep.ing?

I'd prefer to wait forever and ever
in radio silence
for my time, my hour,
my turn,
thank you very much.

Not every empty space
has to be filled with Noise!
Scents!
Lights!
Additives! Spice!
Cicadas!

Our souls need space
rest
blank
white

"How can I help you?"

08.13.20

Note: *The Highly Sensitive Person*, by Elaine N. Aron, Ph.D., is a book that has been invaluable to me in understanding my sensitive nature.

Old Folks Home

All of our venerable elderly
tucked away in facilities,
weighed down w/years,
wishing to be elsewhere
w/their marbles.

Or maybe it doesn't matter to them
where they lay their weary old heads,
or what day it is.

We mourn
and do our best,
standing outside of their windows
on our fancy phones,

Trying to nudge
a smile
from old bones,

Watching with alarm (!),
our vulnerable,
sweet mothers
w/tissue emanating from every conceivable pocket

And grumpy old fathers
w/unkempt eyebrows & &
nothing to do,
going downhill,
in their wheelchairs equipped w/footrests,
over rocks & roots,

moving w/gravity
&
inevitability
toward
the sunset,
toward (we pray)
the warm,
shining figure
of Jesus.

Wave good-bye.

08.13.20

"So do not fear, for I am with you; do not be dismayed,
for I am your God. I will strengthen you and help you;
I will uphold you with my righteous right hand."

-Isaiah 41.10 (NIV)

Butterfly

for Mom

Like a butterfly
under glass,
we wait—working bravely
behind Plexiglas®
or sheltering in place—
for cases
to recede
& life—Abundant
Life!—
to resume.

On her way to get coffee this morning,
in her burnt orange Kia Soul,
Mom encounters a swarm of Monarch butterflies,
too many to number.

As she passes through the orange swarm,
some of them
don't make it; their children & grandchildren will journey on—

...

Grandma sits in her blue-gray Broda® chair
(echoing the color of her home, since departed from),
covered by soft blankets & her daughters' love,
eyes closed, sometimes
opening her good eye: The world is much too bright!
        Sometimes aware of familiar life moving & circulating
around her—waiting for her grand, loving metamorphosis—

08.17.20

Model Daughter

Mom persists in caring for her Mother,
even though Grandma,
due to her dementia—
or maybe because it's hard to be away
from the comforts of home, living with strangers
and eating subpar food—
went through a mean phase.

Mom persists,
even though she
wasn't the favorite daughter.

...

All told, Mom,
more than anyone else,
has been a constant
in her Mom's vulnerable later life;

Mom modeling
how she would like to be cared for
in her later years.

...

It's a lot
to live up to
for a daughter who
doesn't always return
texts and who never
answers her phone.

08.31.20

Nun Sighting

Today, driving through the park,
we witness a line of nuns walking—surely and without
hurry—
uphill,
wearing black habits,
black veils down to their undefined
waists
& simple silver pendants,
featuring Mary, O clement Mother,
at their pale necks.

I (having a small nun obsession) wave exuberantly;
the good sisters wave back,
their smiling, bright shining,
unadorned faces
a delight
and a welcome sight.

Today's obvious highlight.

The sunny, clement fall weather, another highlight.

See: God is kind!

10.07.20

"The loving-kindness of the Lord fills the whole earth."

-Psalm 33.5, "The Psalter," *Book of Common Prayer*

Today, I Cross Paths with a Fox/Journal Therapy

On my way this afternoon,
I stop in my tracks for a red fox,
crossing the crosswalk
all civilized.

The fox—
a welcome anomaly in my workday—
while accompanied by a grand tail—
looks thin & scrappy,
poor fellow.

I want to introduce myself
& feed him/her my arm,
or maybe some worms.

Like Dad, I keep a jar of (unsalted) peanuts in my glove box.

...

Why, pray tell, does compassion well up in me
for hungry animals
more than for my fellow hungry people in need
of succor?

...

I have never known
the hopeless pounding of
hunger—or something beyond hunger—

...

Napoléon's army,
retreating from Moscow,
frozen to the bone and famished,
carved off horses' hindquarters—
the horses yet alive!

Dad, in dire straits and self-sufficient,
never took charity (as I remember, and to his credit,
we always had enough).

08.18.20

"She stretcheth out her hand to the poor; yea, she reacheth forth
her hands to the needy."

-Proverbs 31.20 (KJV)

Gertrude Groundhog

On seeing or sensing Dog,
Gertrude Groundhog comically & rapidly dashes for her very
life—a pillow stuffed w/squirrels on a flat bed of wheels—
to her secure
quiet
cool
home.

...

Soon & very soon,
Grande Dame Gertrude
will gladly arise
to eat clover
dandelions
raspberries
grubs
in the hot sun,
once again.

07.30.20

Perspective

Seventeen-year-old
Joni Eareckson Tada—
the world her oyster—
estimated the water
to be deeper
and dove
straight into a sandbar,
breaking her graceful,
giraffe-long neck,

Severing her tough,
delicate,
ribbon snake-like
spinal cord

And rendering her
a quadriplegic.

Seventy-year-old Joni,
whom we have all
come to know and love,
says that there are more
important things
than able legs.

Soon & very soon,
Joni will walk like a flamingo
& run like a lioness.

I can almost make her out,
running on the soft sand,

waves nearly lapping
her soft flexing feet.

08.04.20

"Feet, what do I need you for when I have wings to fly?"

-Frida Kahlo

Walking is Good for the Soul

MY OTHER CAR
IS A PAIR OF BOOTS

-bumper sticker

People have discovered
the simple joy
of walking,
in quarantine.

Families and friend pods
enjoy nightly walks
& dog owners extend their walks
to the happy surprise
of their dogs' tails.

*

I knew an active older woman
who ritually walked in the good way
3 miles every day—rain/shine—
listening to inspirational cassette tapes
on her Walkman.

I aim to follow
in the footsteps
of this dear old woman,
although 1 mile (2,000 steps)
is plenty for me
to pray, to think,
to clear my head
& to just be,

my feet moving
in cadence beneath me,
my good dog—
who stops on a dime 53x per walk,
to smell things evident
& unknown—
leading the way home
w/his shiny,
black,
baby gorilla's
nose.

10.05.20

Don't Mind Me

Today, driving to & fro, I maneuvered among
the long-legged Sandhill Cranes—expert stilt walkers, they—
wearing red masks (some rusty, some bright) at their crowns,
crossing the road at their very leisure,
simply & delicately about their creaturely business.

Bless you all.

09.13.20

"Nature does not hurry, yet everything is accomplished."

-Lao Tzu

Grateful

A Priest I heard on the radio recently, tells the story of an old woman he counseled who had had a hard knock life.

The only thing the old woman could possibly think of to be grateful for at present:

indoor plumbing

The old woman in the story must not have had a dog.

...

Our dog, Oscar, snoring behind me in my late Grandpa's (may God rest his soul) old armchair as I write, is a small embodiment of everything good in the world.

Furthermore, the dog park is a microcosm of a happy, healthy, well-functioning society: people greeting each other and each others' dogs with a smile; one lady telling her dog to *"Be polite"*; witnessing another lady's exuberance: "You made a *friend*. I'm so *proud* of you!"; (most) people doing their due diligence & cleaning up after their dogs.

Crazy dog (and cat) people are my kind of people, the *best* kind of people, *right*?

08.10.20

Open Up

In a recent interview with Michael J. Fox, diagnosed with Parkinson's at age 29, he talks about people who have a chronic illness often isolating, to make their worlds as small as possible so that they have less to deal with, but "a dog will open you up."

Michael J. Fox's dog, Gus, has secured his place among the family, and appears in Fox's new memoir, *No Time Like the Future*.

*

Aunt JulieAnne once said that my heart is wide open.

My English professors said that they wanted more.

Currently penning my dogoir, because the world *definitely* needs more books about dogs!

11.17.20

"Gus—great dog and loyal friend, we'll miss you"

-@realmikejfox, Instagram, April 12, 2021

Best Advice

Julia Scarlett Elizabeth Louis-Dreyfus' Mom gave her this advice:

Always have something to look forward to (a minor thing or a major thing).

*

After a morning of putting one's nose to the grindstone & writing, May Sarton looked forward to cleaning out her liquor cabinet.

Getting sh*t done at home makes me happy, too.

*

After a sh*tty shift helping the elderly (God bless them), I look forward to watching an episode of *Gilmore Girls* with a bowl of sea salt potato chips.

My husband, at the end of the day, looks forward to reading a weighty historical tome in his late Dad's old (acquired before I was born) armchair with a big cup of (thoroughly artificially sweetened) decaf & a cookie.

This, or watching an episode of *Star Trek*.*

To each, their own.

08.07.20

*Bramwell has seen every episode of every series of *Star Trek* (725 episodes) multiple times.

Eyes

A middle-aged woman
passes me by,
her eyes narrowing to slits,
homing in on my thin, gauzy,
homemade face covering.

I tell an older friend about this
perceived meanness,
who doesn't give a fig
what people think of her.

Helen cares about:

Feeding the birds,
what she's going to make
herself for dinner,
names of flowers
& her watercolors.

Her sunsets are magical.

*

Mom takes pics of sunsets on her old iPhone
& posts them to Facebook.

They are holy pockets:

Hollows in trees
housing brilliantly-painted
Easter eggs,

the mystic swirl of Mary's womb

08.05.20

"Are not flowers the stars of the earth?"

-Clara Lucas Balfour

✝ JESUS, MARIA ✝

All Eyes (A Google Search)

People wearing face masks are All Eyes like Twiggy; Pluto (minus the big tongue & matching ears); Margaret Keane portraits of children with oversized eyes ("A Boy and His Dog" my fave); the green, 3-eyed squeaky toy aliens in *Toy Story*; the 4 living creatures in Revelation, full of eyes all around & & within.

We are in uncharted territory,
living in unprecedented times:
Wide-eyed, sleepy-eyed, mystified,
terrified.

My dang right eye
won't stop twitching.

While I'd *like* for my big blue eyes to look
like a cartoon character in love's eyes,
like the eyes of Love,
they likely look like Marvin the Martian's
expressly angry eyes
& like a GIF of a teenager who *rolls her eyes* a lot:
She can't help it.

08.13.20

"I will guide you with My eye." (NKJV)

-Psalm 32.8

25

Be Still

Mama deer lookin' thin
& so beautiful, sleek:

She standing there in the road,
her & her giant brown, cinematic eyes:
Audrey Tautou in a double-breasted,
light brown walker coat.

I in my mint green Prius stopped
in the road, waiting on my meek kin
to be on her graceful way.

...

The wondering world is still
in this pregnant pause

...

I say "Hello,"
look to the side of the road,
where a li'l light brown fawn
decorated in white fingerprints, stirs,
safely behind a fence.

I go on my busy way,
trusting that everything is OK,
in the natural order of
dear things on the way.

Amen.

05.18.20

Charlotte

Charlotte, on first meeting me,
said that she knew I was a Christian:
She could see it in my eyes.

Some moments, some words
stick with us for a lifetime.

Charlotte's eyes
are joyful wells of water:
knowing, living, sparkling, hazel.

Her eyes also possess some sort of
sincerity meter with which to suss out
people's sincerity.

...

Charlotte brings people good coffee,
keeps children warm, like a mother hen,
in her large, zippered sweatshirt
and, with her humble, Christ-like husband,
does the work that needs doing.

In another life, a larger life,
my daughter's name would be
Charlotte,
or Violet (Great Grandmother's name).

09.10.20

Somebody

Somebody sits on your heart,
like a song that you can't get out of your head.
You carry him around all day, like a teething child,
like a toothache,
the Holy Spirit pressing upon you from the inside
like a shadow with teeth (not breaking the skin).

You wonder what on earth you (who am I?)
can possibly do
to comfort,
to lessen her pain,
to, at the very least,
let her know that you care (you who are suddenly
chock-full of care!).

If your heart remains open,
your answer will come like a kiss.

Bless

*

08.10.20

Untitled (heartache)

Threatening clouds.
His cancer returned.

Does chaos & double heartache
have to be the theme of *everything*
this year?

I'm sorry.

I'll cry for you:

For your heavy brow,
your beautiful, wormy body,
your disappearing beard
& your loving, photogenic family.

...

08.10.20

"You cannot uncreate me."

-Katy Bowser to cancer, "Eraser," *Now I Lay Me Down To Fight*

Maple, Malt, Virtual Quilt

Aunt Wendy Jo brings her dog, Maple,
who resembles a braided jute rug,
Fozzie Bear, Rowlf the Dog
& a peanut butter cookie,
to visit Grandma at the care center.

Mom, on her regular visits
(when restrictions are not in place),
brings to Grandma:
warm cotton socks & chocolate malts.

Prayers from daughters,
who aren't able to visit,
cover Grandma
like a handmade, virtual* quilt,
each square & shape signifying
a specific, tangible blessing,
wish, emotion, question,
unnamed/uncovered thing.

08.31.20

*"Existing...in essence or effect."

-The Free Dictionary

<Apple>

I, growing a little rounder
(not that sort of round)
by the day
& juicier

A Pink Lady apple
on the flourishing tree,
tart & sweet

Yet fearful—
in my host body—
of Worm
(which could be
soooooooo many impending,
doomy, gloomy, zoomy things
at any given moment—

The teeth of anxiety*
keep you stuck,
stalled in your horse stall,
getting you (body & soul) exactly nowhere,
lovely people.

*A*choo**

08.13.20

*Nod to Joy Harjo (*Crazy Brave*).

The Maker of Trees

for Dad

The perfect forest,
over time,
has been disturbed,
to allow space for:

A small seminary,
established to grow sun-loving priests,
following their high calling.

The surrounding, living trees
do not hold grudges.

They stand proud.
Shelter and cover
and provide homes
       & hiding places
for those who need them, like
birds of the air, following
their high calling.

...

The trees wave gracefully, sway
in the soft breeze,
unaware of their
bold beauty & tough,
delicate greenery.

The framework of a leaf, *I mean.*

And: Strong and solid old trees
stand motionless,
take up space,
ring upon ring,
age after age,
abiding without apology.

When storm or disease strikes
      & befalls a tree,
or a branch,
it succumbs willingly,
always at peace with its Maker.

...

We aren't made to hang onto things,
wrongs, cavities, dead limbs for a lifetime.

We're made to be free, indeed,
as children of love, swinging, laughing high & higher—
unencumbered as trees—

07.30.20

MAY THE FOREST BE WITH YOU

He Held the Door

Coming out of the post office today,
an old man holds the door for me—
the man and the door in polite cooperation—
like he's always done for the ladies:
He was raised well.

A little bit of kindness and normalcy
(in the midst of a whole lot of cantankerousness
and division and partitions and mass shootings, terrifying
etcetera) goes a long way, these days:

"Thank you, Sir."

*

07.27.20

The Opposite of Twister®

For people standing in line
at the post office,
brightly colored circles:
red, blue, yellow, green,
have been placed
on the colorless linoleum tiles,
precisely 6 feet apart,
like Twister,
but with no personal contact
and no fun.

...

(For some—
extroverts like my brother,
Jeremiah-pie-a, who thrive on
being with people and being busy,
in community—
living in a bubble
is their worst nightmare.
They chafe against it,
the bubble.)

(And for others—
introverts
who thrive on the quiet—Hi—
it's kind of a dream
come true: We win,
somewhat guiltily.)

08.02.20

The Public Library Looks Like a Hospital Ward

Most of the library
is cordoned off
like a crime scene, or
a museum under renovation.

Patrons are not free to roam
or touch the good stuff.

The Circulation staff and Librarians
are safely masked & & gloved,
Nurses following strict protocol,
behind bulletproof sneeze guards.

A Detroit banker hands me—
loyal patron & book junkie—
my powdered & sterilized,
held baby books.

I try not to cry.

Some generous libraries have done away with
fines.

Some Little Free Libraries have been stocked
with non-perishable goods & sundries.

"Take what you need. Leave what you can."

09.23.20

36

Control Freak

Katy Perry,
pop star & first time mother,
has had to learn how
to relinquish
control
& chill
during Covid.

Katy is happy
& beyond excited
for what is to come,
for who is coming:

She sings to her baby girl,
as many mothers naturally do,
in utero.

...

Orlando Bloom,
already chill,
is excited, too.

He misses his teacup poodle,
Mighty (a gift from Perry),
finely tattooed over his heart.

He is mighty to save us—
control freak (I wonder how Kate + 8
is doing in quarantine),
calm in a storm,

or somewhere in between.

08.15.20

Instagram post by UNICEF on Aug. 26:

Katy has her baby girl, Daisy Dove Bloom.

*

I'm Not OK; Are You OK?

A prolonged panic attack
which refreshes every day—a
loop of panic—
can't be good for one
sensitive soul.

I need to find a suitable hole
(no way I'm staying at a hotel),
or an oversized shoe,
in which to lay my horribly
dizzy (is it a brain tumor?)
(Unbalanced crystals
in my inner ear?)
head.

Maybe I'll fly
to our family's
cabin in the woods
and subsist
on books
and bowls of oatmeal
w/brown sugar
and rest
in its nest (its humble loft),
but for its community of mice.

P.S. I would ask how you're doing/feeling
but maybe you don't know,
or you don't wish to say, because the world
is not OK, so how could you *possibly*
be OK, or whatever.

Which is totally OK.

Note to Mom: I'm *OK*.

And, yes, I'm taking
Vitamin D.

Also: zinc, olive leaf oil,
Vitamin C & turmeric.

08.23.20

cabin pic

I Just Want to Float/Mom Visits

Sometimes, I just want to float
in a blow-up Swan,
be still with her floating
—beside me but not *right*
beside me—in a blow-up Swan,
us floating together,
unhurried,
unworried,
drinking our decaf iced lattés
(hers with oat milk,
mine with almond milk),
together.

...

I don't feel like
being sniffed
at all times
by her well-meaning,
drug-sniffing
Shepherd's
nose.

I wish her pretty, blue-green laser eyes
pointing directly at
her target: my heart,
would focus beyond the foreground
to the middle distance, or the far East,
or at least
beyond me.

I'd rather not say
how I'm feeling, today, OK?

Remember
that I'm always and ever reticent
except in writing (turns out
I'm an open book)?

...

A friend needs
a day's buffer,
on either side,
of visiting family.

P.S. Love you, Mom!

09.05.20

Today, We Happen Upon a Cat/Poetry is All Around Us

Today on our walk,
we happen upon an orange tabby cat,
nestled in the grass,
a little removed from the trail,
resting underneath
a sunbeam.

The cat looks at me Wide-Eyed
like she has just seen a ghost, or an Angel,
or a wild animal & like I had best get thee
      & my rude dog away,
if I know what's good for me
      & my rude dog,
disturbing her quiet calm.

I don't usually have fond feelings
towards cats (I'm allergic)
but I immediately like this cat
who reminds me of
myself (save my dog-loving self).

...

When I was a baby, reportedly,
our orange tabby cat, Buffy,
slept curled up in my crib.

09.24.20

"The wolf and the lamb shall graze together; [the dog and the cat will lie down together]..."

-Isaiah 65.25 (ESV) (words in square brackets mine)

43

Mean Aunt/Journal Therapy #2

I walk by a gaggle
of kids in our multiplex,
piled in the hammock,
which kids look at me
like I'm their mean aunt,
a total destroyer of their fun.

When did I become allergic to kids,
see them solely as noise-makers
and disturbances
to personal peace and order

(*dons pink noise-cancelling headphones*)?

When did I become a grumpy,
ugly, warty, poorly tattooed old lady with a 5 o'clock
shadow,
staying away from all forms of sugar (including fruit)
& brandishing a cane
(on the un-childlike inside)?

When did I become the opposite of fun,
pointing my pale arm in the opposite direction
of the warm, welcoming Heart of Jesus?

(*Releases the kids' pet frogs,
formerly held hostage in a plastic tub,
just as Jesus instructed me to do*)

...

In my defense,
as said, we live in a multiplex
with noisy rug rats
on either side,
all the livelong summer day,
all the livelong quarantined day,
and I need quiet
like air.

P.S. It is not lost on me
that I'm surrounded by good, flourishing people
and I'm/we're safe (because neighbor watches out
for neighbor) (even when one neighbor is antisocial
and only talks to her dog),
living at a small Episcopal seminary
in the wilds of Wisconsin.

08.31.20

On Wearing a Mask

Wearing a mask
feels like looking thru
a fogged up glass,
trying to make out
details of
a face.

Like wearing
ear plugs while
conversing w/your neighbor,
loving your neighbor,
thru a fence.

Like smelling the roses
w/an unfriendly clothes pin
pinching yr nostrils.

Like breathing
thru
3 paper straws.

You're the drama queen.

Note: This poem has nothing to do with politics.

07.31.20

Vitriol

People in public
not wearing masks,
while more comfortable in the chaos,
are met with vitriol
from passersby
who view themselves
as veritable Kindness Martyrs
and those god-forsaken people
walking & breathing potentially lethal droplets
among us, not bothering to wear masks/
protective face coverings/face shields + N95 masks
(breath),
as unkind, unschooled, right wing
nutcases, selfish
to their very rotten cores,
furthermore, as pariahs and lepers
deserving of mean girl looks & &
Extra   Wide   Berths.

The mask goes *over your nose*, Bertha!!

09.07.20

𝕿𝖍𝖚𝖌 𝕷𝖎𝖋𝖊

Maskne/Forbearance

acne mechanica

Wearing a mask
must trump
vanity.

Kindness
must trump
maskne.

God bless you
and me
& our spots.

Also: surgeons,
dentists
& nail techs,
our mask & maskne
forebears.

*

Reward for wearing
my mask today:

4 sugar-free gummy bears
(you're welcome
to the green ones.)

(Note: "Sugar-free" doesn't mean
marijuana.)

08.23.20

Matchy-matchy

Does your cloth mask
match your outfit,
like my bone white mask
with tiny blue florals
& li'l green leaves
matches my navy blouse
with puff sleeves,
matches my moss green capris,
matches my lettuce-trim ankle socks
with tiny pink florals,
matches my oblong barrettes
inset with "pearls"?

While some women like to wear lipstick
under their masks,
just for themselves,
other women have given up
on makeup, entirely, allowing their skin to breathe.

You don't need to put on your face—
your face is your face. Stop. Touching. Your. Face.

Maybe a little under-eye concealer.

(Mom says that the dark circles under my eyes
are from lack of eating red meat.)

(And, obviously, from lack of sleep.)

...

Interestingly, some men
(of the Anglican/Episcopal/Catholic variety)
like to dress up
for church in their living rooms.

08.29.20

Church in the Time of Quarantine

In today's video update, our consistent Priest friend—
wearing a white button-down, against the sky blue backdrop
of a bright upper room in his home, a portion of a white
ceiling fan visible—resembles a cloud, wearing glasses.

Please drop off school supplies at the parish hall.

Happy Birthday, Herbert Hoover!

08.10.20

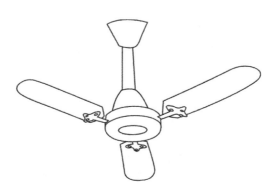

It's been cold and rainy for days.

A dark clump of cloud positions itself above
my dull crown, making everything
gray, stale, stagnant,
cold, colorless, lackluster.

Words—words read, written words—
all fall flat as pancakes—
minus the warm, plump feelings
pancakes provoke.

x

My migraine drags on, day after day,
each day trudging (keep going)
through a never-ending trail (keep trudging)
of molasses.

He is with me—a pillar of Cumulus cloud by day
and by night, a pillar of campfire—

He feeds me gingerbread cookies
& smiles on me
in my crummy melancholy.

Melancholia

09.10.20

Melancholy (Psychology) (*archaic*): a gloomy character, thought
to be caused by too much black bile.

-*The Free Dictionary*

One Groundhog

for Dr. B, who lives patiently

One groundhog
ushered
underground,
under the cool,
dark ground,
where at least
it is safe
&
quiet,
to think
and to ponder
one's home,
one's room,
one's groundhog
sisters and brothers
&
when at last,
it is safe
& when, in a little while, it is time:

A plan put in motion
to exit & emerge
from captivity
a better,
sounder, stronger,
fitter, mightier
creature.

07.19.20

National Read a Book Day

for Ryan

Whilst being treated for cancer,
he brings a book with him everywhere,
like Rory Gilmore of *Gilmore Girls*.

And not just any book—books
on difficult topics facing us today:

Race and gender roles,
neglected populations, justice,
the role of the church.

He grows stronger interiorly,
day by day,
book by book,
while fighting mightily
for his balding, bruised body
taking a beating.

09.06.20

My Bookworm

More books, less Netflix

My husband, Bramwell the Bookworm,
has made a spreadsheet of all of the books
(he's on a Napoléon kick, momentarily sidestepped
to read about the doctrine of the Holy Spirit)
that he wishes to read
on vacation.

So far this year,
B has read
84 books.
His goal for 2020
is to read
100 books.

He says that reading is relaxing,
like some think that fishing is relaxing,
golfing is relaxing, or
knitting is relaxing.

Can you *even*
and: I aim to be more like B,
devouring books like
Cavatappi Bolognese.

Staying up well past my bedtime
to read one more chapter,
just one more chapter.

10.05.20

Glittery Gold Star: B finished his 100th book on Dec. 5, 2020!

KEEP CALM
AND
READ ON

...

KEEP CALM
AND
PRAY ON

...

KEEP CALM
AND
CALL YOUR
MOM

Illiterate/Hate Mail/R.I.P.

It must be hard for the illiterate among us
during this pandemic, especially,
to navigate shopping
with its mosaic of Covid rules:

Signs plastered all over storefronts
w/varying information & unique—
some might say ridiculous—requirements.

Before entering a store with a friend,
besides putting on a compliant *mask* as an executive order-
abiding citizen, at the moment,
I'm required to choose 1 of 6 crazy floral-and/or-fruity-
scented
hand sanitizers
with which to sanitize my hands.

I stare at the hand sanitizers for a long while
like a deer in headlights with a sensitivity to scents,
or somebody with low blood oxygen
levels.

A bumblebee rests
on my nose wire
like I'm a sunflower.

A friend pokes tiny holes
in her disposable mask,
like we poked holes in jar lids,
so that our caterpillars could breathe,
as kids.

...

We're so sorry
that your glittery, golden breath
was cut short,
George Perry Floyd, Jr.,
father and mentor,
and so much more,
and so many more.

08.21.20

Note: On April 20th, 2021, Derek Chauvin, former police officer in Minneapolis, is found guilty of all charges in George Floyd's death, providing justice in small measure.

Stunning Sunset

A description of today's sunset, by a beautiful Black
matriarch from Milwaukee, whom I care for:

Crucified Copper

07.31.20

...

How are you doing?
Let me play you a sad song:
Lady Day's "Strange Fruit."

(Haiku)

Saddled

Saddled with to-do's
& obligations & stray gray hairs
& news cycles & new developments
& work & the full-time job of having a smart phone
(breath),
one's addled brain can scarcely rest,
one's restless, indefatigable body can scarcely
be still,
long enough to go deep,
dig deeper still:
     to the core
     to the soul
     to the essential self
     to the essential, magical, mystical self
     to the underground hiding place
     where God & poems live

     ...

     seeds

07.22.20

When My Student Loan is Paid Off/Bernie Tried

I'll write little poems
and read YA novels
and walk my little dog, rain or shine
and sleep well through the night season
and wear house dresses (w/pockets) through the day
and start my Wisconsin fashion blog
and pray, really pray
and sip my coffee
and help the elderly,
to live their remaining days well.

...

I'm aware that my student loan will be paid off...
approximately never. But one can dream dreams
of heart patch pockets, healthcare for all
and getting an M.F.A. in Poetry.

07.13.20

Note: Thanks to my parents, who have always helped their
artistic daughter in money (and other) matters. And to all
parents of artists, who have allowed their children to be
who they were created to be, and to do what they do, and
to find their way, with your kind help. I pray that your
reward will someday come back to you, if it hasn't already.

43

I'm graying,
drying out at my root,
using up lotion
like it's going out of style.

Eyebrows thinning,
breasts drooping,
veins popping,
Help, I can only remember 2 things at once.

..

"Don't get old," old folks say.

Because bodily & mentally,
mentally & bodily,
they know it's an irreversible,
downhill
slope (redemption our only hope)
(& maybe a good oil-free wrinkle cream
for the yet acne-prone).

...

Old folks also tell me
that I'm still young
and to enjoy life.

They wonder
why on earth I don't have children.

Who will help me when I am old?

Who will advocate for me in medical matters?

Who will pluck my coarse, dark chin hairs?!

...

I'm a mist
& if I'm a morning mist,
I want to spend my time writing.

Or, maybe I'll change my mind—
Chloë Stevens Sevigny had her first child,
Vanja, at 45.

07.23.20

I. Trapped

Four-to-six days per month (usually, rudely),
my body betrays me.

Does its damn thing,
despite me.

I sit with my green flax seed heating bag, my BFF,
in my late Grandpa's (God rest his soul) old armchair
and watch horror/Hallmark movies (depending on my mood)
on my purple Dell laptop (I'm open
to sponsorship, if nothing else).

Nothing and nobody
can help me
with that ordinary red disease.

Get away from me.
I love you, I do.

The world has gone to pot.
Who will save us and our racked, bloody bodies?

...

My husband is a saint
during this most trying time.

The woman in the Bible with the issue,
issuinggg of blood is close to me.

For those of you who are trapped in your broken bodies 24/7,
I'm so sorry.

09.21.20

64

II. Trapped: Happy Halloween!

Possibly, in a few months to a year
or, in a few weeks to half a year
or: momentarily,
we may have a safe vaccine
for Covid-19.

Then we can all (or, like, 51% of us) come out of our houses,
wearing our Sunday bests
& play Ring-Around-the-Rosie;

The nursery rhyme having various interpretations:
one referencing the Black Death,
another referring to courtship,
flowering love & joy.

As of yet, we're still in the dark,
gathered in our basements,
waiting for the tornado/Frankenstein virus to pass...
praying for a medical miracle...

In the meantime, neighbors have garishly
decorated their homes & front yards for Halloween,
sparing no expense:

Giant Spiders in great cottony webs,
menacing witches, levitating ghosts,
        comically posed plastic bones, on swings,
a pirate ship with a skeleton crew (ha)
        & kitschy orange
                & black plastic flamingOs.
09.28.20

III. Who Knows When

My clenching body
will cease its clenching
& flowing & exploding
& perfectly ruining & awfulizing
& staining my life.

Who knows when
this hell-bent pandemic
will be behind us
or will it ever be with us,
mutating like the flu into differing god-awful strains??*

The "Spanish" flu
had 4 successive waves.

...

We carry around uncertainty
in our bodies,
in our bellies, our breasts,
in our teeth,
in our homes,
in our world.

One perimenopausal woman must carry on—
rain or shine,
desert or downpour or damn pandemic,
fountain of
frowning (not flowering!) (not empowering!) blood,
or none,
for months on end,

count the months &
& always be prepared, like Mom said—.

Things won't be this way forever.

Someday, *Le Sigh*, it'll all be
over & done,
our suffering & wondering complete,
our uteruses & souls made sound & whole—
free of disease, of sin & PMS,
of doubt & dread & unrest—

Life all abundant & flourishing in & around us forever—
Won't that rock?
Amen!

...

Interestingly, some women
use diluted period blood
for plant fertilizer,
utilizing its nitrogen,
phosphorus & potassium.

What do you know,
it's/i'm good for something
symbiotic.

08.09.20

*It's what viruses
do.

Survivors

The beautiful, old-growth California Redwoods
—their thick trunks stretching to the sky—
have been burned again,
some destroyed,
their royal crowns burnt off.

But Redwoods are remarkably resilient trees
like us sentient beings, marked
w/scars & grit,
from our years of standing & fighting
(we're all fighting our own battles, doing our best,
or not),
every day enduring
& breathing, just breathing,
grounded on this earth—
sometimes a greenly paradise,
sometimes hell-on-earth—
yet stretching Skyward! Just as we were made to do—be

Help us to turn over new leaves
—forsaking the drab old life—
& Grow Up, folks!!

08.25.20

Oliver

I forgot that I love him. We were in each other's lives for a long season (as caregiving goes), even if we didn't say much. I made him good brunches: scrambled eggs & bacon (crispy) and English muffins with butter & jam, and Folgers® 1/2 caff, which coffee he politely accepted. We watched the birds, and the news (on a rotating loop). We read our respective books in adjacent armchairs (I honorably occupying his late wife's armchair), our antennas tuned to the wild world outside his large windows.

While the multitude of field mice in Oliver's* old home, which he helped to build, didn't startle him, they never failed to startle! me!

Oliver's successful son—a helicopter parent—loved his Dad fiercely, left a dizzying multitude of Post-it® notes about the house, treated the caregivers rudely, sometimes nicely.

One sad day, Oliver was diagnosed with the big "C" (compounding his health problems). And I couldn't deal.

One CG (Cute Girl) can only handle so much. And, so, she moves on to the next client, or takes a break, works in kitchens, chopping food & washing dishes.

...

A year later, I return. To my surprise, Oliver is doing well— his tall, skeletal frame is filled in. His care is a well-oiled machine, thanks to his capable, only son, who humbly put himself in the caregiver rotation.

Among the rotating caregivers, I don't think Oliver remembers me.

I make the coffee in the percolator too strong, like the Swedes.

In the slim space between the counter and the large, shiny new refrigerator, I find a dead mouse stuck to the floor!

x

Perhaps if I lowered my mask, Oliver might remember our quiet, calm days together. Although, yesterday is a blur.

...

05.09.21

*Name, etc. details, changed.

Annoyed in 2020

"The Lord puts up with me."

-St. Theresa of Ávila

Among us are many helpers;
many people fighting for justice,
heroes fighting mega fires and not stopping,
people giving from their abundances,
persons peacefully protesting.

Among us are many people
living their daily lives
in such a way that their light shines
before women & men,
like those feminine fireflies:

Dolly Rebecca Parton
Erin Rasberry Napier
Jennifer Anne Garner

Good for them.
We love them.

*

If I'm honest (you best be honest in writing),
I'm over here living my little life in 2020
mostly annoyed at everything and everybody.

Under my stupid mask,
I'm scowling (not smiling and certainly not "smizing")
& & under my cheap, oversized, foggy sunglasses,
my curated Kardashian brow is

furrowed.

Where has my
little light, my shine, sheen,
gone?

...

It's still here,
deep within
my newly acquired,
quarantine fat layers:
a bro-ken
heart night-light
weapon
that glows
when I'm not
looking.

And it's here,
in this little book of
personal, pandemic,
humble (the humblest),
self-published poems
(my heart's small contribution),
I
(miffed)
hope
?

09.27.20

R.I.P. Ruth Bader Ginsburg, 87 (After a long battle with cancer,
and tirelessly fighting for women's rights and gender equality,
etc., RBG died on Sept. 18th, 2020.)

Grocery Shopping Blues

After sterilizing one's cart
(if it has not already been sterilized & is sticky & strong-of-smell),
one shopper
must get in & get out.

All of the sensuality of grocery shopping is
gone.

No more handling of Granny Smith apples till the perfect
one
is found.

No more smelling fresh loaves of sourdough bread
or
vented bags of dark roast coffee beans.

No more people-watching
or
casually engaging with people—
one must keep her marked distance
from
masked shoppers—follow the arrows or else →   →

Even eye contact is weird:
Don't look at me.
What are you looking at.
Hi.

...

For many Midwestern guys, it's not that bad.
This is how they usually go about shopping:

It's a Mission,
not a meandering
amusement.

And, some of us evolved, adaptable types are somehow
going with the flow,
making & offering up our own sourdough loaves.

Many overwhelmed mothers
have fallen head over heels
for grocery pickup & delivery.

But for one serious shopper,
what used to be a ritual, therapeutic experience,
is now the opposite:

empty shelves
blank faces
stony hearts

...

Finally,
when one frustrated & exhausted &
sapped shopper
finishes the race—
after removing her face mask,
sucking in air, sighing within herself
& & sanitizing her hands—

She may reward herself
with a Party Size bag of
salt & vinegar potato chips
& Hillsong Worship played LOUD,
in the safety of her Corolla.

08.01.20

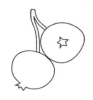

Bad Spots

I was surprised to learn
that not everybody cuts out
the bad spots of bananas.

Some people eat
the bad spots,
so as not to waste banana.

Some of us, for various reasons,
remain in bad marriages,
work at jobs we hate,
forget about
our wants and needs,
our loves,
for a lifetime.

...

Following an EEG,
my older friend, Mary Ann,
thin of hair,
had bald spots
where the electrodes
were pasted
onto her scalp.

It's OK to cry.

10.11.20

Dogs are Supposed to be Spoiled

Some old folks whom I work for have dogs,
very loyal dogs with great names
like Lady Jane and Love,
Happy, Sugar and Baguette.

While the dogs don't
get enough exercise,
they get treats all of the time
because their owners often
don't remember
when their respective dogs
last had a treat (oh dear).

The dogs also get all of the attention & affection
in the world
from their people
who stay in one place all day,
pretty much.

<3

11.07.20

I Waited All Damn Day

For the Plumber to show up,
so that I could go for a walk outside,
and get some sun on the whites of my eyeballs.

...

Update: The Plumber went to the wrong unit,
couldn't find anything wrong,
like the President.

08.10.20

JESUS 2020

thrifted Jesus

Something

Something fat & long
at the familiar trailhead...
as we draw closer,
we find: one Groundhog Survivor—
after Pest Control had their way—
who quickly points & wheels himself
back from whence he
came.

○

Sometimes, I see Something
blurry, golden,
in my right eye's
lost peripheral vision.

Oscar, his poor, old,
brown penny eyes filmy,
sometimes thinks
a potato chip bag blowing,
a leaf pile,
is Something.

...

Last night,
Oscar was on High Alert
re: Something
in the bedroom doorway...

Dogs do know things.

We only have today.   07.16.20

Sideways Dance of the Sandhill Crane

Leaving for work this morning, I pass a Sandhill Crane beside the road who does not sensibly turn her light gray/brown bustle & walk/run away but performs a sideways dance w/her connecting-lines-for-legs, that makes me laugh.

Likewise, some clever, flexible citizens among us have pivoted their way to success.

10.10.20

2-D Priest

Our Priest, in person,
is On and in his element:
jovial & happy to be among his people.

Virtually, our Priest
is a different kettle of fish.

He's familiar,
like a distant relative—
his nose is larger
than I remember.

Does he see me
in my PJ's?
Does he hear my faithful dog,
barking at the moon,
in the background?

He sees everybody at once
like God, our Father,
and nobody,
save his reflection
in the video camera's monitor.

Our Priest stands alone
(his sheep currently quarantined
yet still in his purview),
save his Organist
& most excellent Wife.

We miss them, in person,
they with us.

Our Priest is different in 2-D
& there is a pesky glare
on his glasses;
Our mega-talented Organist
is halved (like the stage magic trick),
to fit in more candles: lit.

09.21.20

Church in the Parking Lot

Quiet, calm, still, orderly,
weird.

Our Priest outfitted in green chasuble,
for Ordinary Time—
although this time is anything but ordinary—
black Birkenstock® clogs
and black mask:
a Kindness Crusader.

Easily distracted, I watch pigeons land
on the roof & upper windows of the church,
envious of their close proximity to the church.

It's nice to be nearer our church,
if not *in* our household, the church.

And it's nice to see our 2-D Priest
in the flesh (Charlie Brown in a Stormy Kromer cap)
& his mini-me son, trained up in the Lord
and in the Church, wearing a surplice,
his hair a mop.

I should talk:
My last haircut was at the beginning of *March*.

A black-gloved hand carefully reaches
into our car window,
to give to us
the germ-free Body of Christ,
the super-substantial Bread of Life,

which I haven't partaken of
in *forever*. Ravenous,
I power the window up,
eat it up & am Revived.

09.27.20

"For the Bread of God is He who comes down from Heaven
and gives Life to the world."

-John 6.33 (ESV) (liberty with caps my own)

Dog on Parade

On our walk this afternoon,
we meet a woman *rolling*
her dog—medium-sized, black & white
w/pointy ears at attention!!—
on a modified stroller contraption,
having a flat, carpeted bed.

The poor dog had recently
been hit by a car
and his/her hind legs
are immobile,
sporting hot pink casts.

The dog—sitting pretty in her parade float—
barks "Hello!" or
"The *indignity*!" at passersby.

When you, a spectator in our weird, wide world,
smile big!!
& wish to cry,
all at once.

...

Oscar, our only child,
thinks that the world
revolves around him.

Sometimes, I
have to remind myself,
like a child,

that the world does not,
in fact,
revolve around me.

I am but a (stylish) speck.

10.11.20

Once, riding along with an older friend,
we suddenly stopped
at the sight of a young boy of 7 or 8,
walking alone on the road,
he & his stick.

Rolling down her window,
my friend asked the boy
where his mother was
and other questions pertaining
to his well-being.

Before driving off,
my friend said to the boy:

"Be careful. We *need* you."

You and I, strangers in this land,
are made of matter
& so much more:

Strong bones, muscles,
sinews &
& wiings (fitted, for now,
for earthly exercise).

God loves you to bits &

You Matter, Son, Daughter

10.07.20

"'For I know the plans I have for you,'" declares the Lord, 'plans to prosper you and not to harm you, plans to give you hope and a future.'"

-Jeremiah 29.11, 12 (NIV)

...

"For in you, O Lord, have I fixed my hope."

-Psalm 38.15, "The Psalter," BCP

...

"But if we hope for what we do not see, we wait for it with patience."

-Romans 8.25 (ESV)

Oscar Takes a New Route

Today, having walked the same route
with Oscar for, like, 5 years,
at roughly the same time of day,
he wanted to go a different way—
baffling but OK.

There is always another way—
other options, different directions,
new-found perspectives and POVs (I promise!).

And where no options or ways
can be sniffed out and found
(and I don't mean weed),
please ask for help and/or
create an opportunity,
make a way.

Who knows (life is full of surprises)?—

Some kind of wonder (a taco truck, maybe)
may be just around the corner—

10.11.20

A Good Friend

Today, I met a man, John,
who has stepped in to care
for his friend, Henry,
in the last stages
of his life, in his lived-in,
intimate home.

John grew up on a dairy farm
in Wisconsin
and is not grossed out
by much.

He uses his big, able,
bare hands
to clean up sh*t
and to make fried eggs
& toast—cut on the bias—
for his friend.

John is an atheist
and one of the kindest people
I've had the pleasure of meeting.

What I witnessed today
was good,
was gold.

Love, in action,
morning and evening,
without fail,
like the sun,

the moon.

**

To my surprise,
over black coffee
& a little whole milk,
John asks his friend, Henry,
also non-religious,
to put in a good word for him
on the other side.

I'll put in a good word
for John, here.

10.18.20

The Plumber Shows Up

"All shall be well, and all
manner of thing shall be well."

-Julian of Norwich

The Plumber who resembles Ed Harris
w/slices of pizza tattooed
on his respective forearms,
who loves dogs & whose phone rings
with a gentle guitar riff,
expertly fixed our bathtub's overflow drain
(a damaged gasket of which had caused water to leak
into the ½ bath below)
& all is well at the moment,
domestically speaking, at least,
in case you were left wondering,
your eyes & & maybe your fists
raised to the misty ceiling/sky—

...

08.12.20

Happy National Coffee Day

Not to sound like a Pollyanna
or a Drew Blythe Barrymore,
but in troubled times,
in our troubled land,
it helps to focus on the Good:
on routine & simple pleasures,
like Coffee:

An iced latté
with 3 shots of Git-R-Done
& almond milk.

Recently, my sweet husband
got me a Starbucks gift card
that replenishes
in $10 increments—lucky me!

In the morning
when I rise
give me Jesus
(and coffee)

It helps to be a mug-half-full sort of person,
that is: an optimist & a realist—wearing rose-colored
sunglasses whilst balancing a Biology textbook
& a YETI rambler tumbler—
in a global pandemic.

Do you want to be a bitter Betty,
or change for the better?

09.29.20

Rise & Shine & Survive

His mercies are new,
unfolding for us like a Peony
or a "Peo-Knee" tattoo
// a double rainbow = hope & promise x2,
every morning.

One day at a time.
One step, tap at a time.

Today has enough
worries & furies,
troubles & foibles,
of its own, man, woman.

...

If you need a mental health day,
a pause,
take one:

Applause

Productivity isn't everything—
we're not made of metal.

Please, Lord, equip me with more mettle
& mithril:

Joan of Arc x Enola Holmes x Mary (sturdy, ethereal & glittery)

09.29.20

Look Up, Child*

Hating groundhogs
& President Trump
& Trumpsters
& idiots not bothering
        to wear masks (*grimace*)
& fireworks
& tattoos
& & broccoli,
is one's prerogative.

But how about we turn our foci,
turn our faces & our hearts
toward something more positive,
like Dogs
Dark Chocolate
Delphiniums
Fresh Air
Gladioli
Oprah
Jesus.

08.13.20

*Nod to Singer, Lauren Ashley Daigle, *Look Up Child*.

SPREAD HUMMUS NOT HATE

95

Invitation

Our spiritual presences
have been requested, online,
for an upcoming ordination
on Saturday, the fifth of December,
in the year of our Lord two thousand twenty,
at eleven o'clock in the morning.

snicker

Spiritual Communion

yawn

Some say that American Christians
are soft.

waft

11.15.20

Phantom Mask

Wait, am I
wearing a mask
or has my lost leg
or my golden arm
come back
to haunt me?

Alexa?

08.23.20

R.I.P.

People die
When it's their time,
Yet it's always
A shocking thing.
It just is.
Life,
Death,
In the blink of an eye,
Or, a long, drawn-out good-bye.

09.01.20

We'll Miss Your Ebullience

1 family unit,
at once,
could go up
to view him
—a white rose
in hand—
his face
overdone
(they did their best)
(I'm doing my best here)
(not that everything's about me, obviously)
(the reader too strongly agrees),
his body
too still

His soul flown
elsewhere—
we know where:

God in him,
reunited.

We'll miss you,
dear ebullient,
rosy-cheeked man.

Maybe you'll
be reunited
with your beard, too,
made more glorious,
a nest for doves,

flying to & fro,
in their missional work.

09.07.20

"Every flower holds the whole mystery in its short cycle,
and in the garden we are never far away from death..."

-May Sarton, *Journal of a Solitude*

Nuns are Dropping Like Flies

In a retirement home in Wisconsin
not too far from us,
w/i a 2-week span,
8 nuns have died of Covid-19.

Most of the nuns
were ripe old ages
and may have been
robust or frail.

At a convent near Milwaukee,
6 elderly sisters
infected w/the virus,
have died.

At a facility near Detroit,
13 sisters carrying the plague,
have passed.

We thank each of the nuns
for their humble service.

...

The remaining nuns—
robust or frail—
are shut up in their rooms,
watching Mass
on closed-circuit TV,
singular hearts stricken,
perishable nightgowns drying,

eyes open,
dreaming of flying

12.18.20

Note: Concerning numbers, news reports vary somewhat.

"For the perishable must be clothed with the imperishable, and the mortal with immortality...Death has been swallowed up in victory."

-1 Corinthians 15.53, 54 (BSB)

Confessional

Today, about my all-important business,
I was interrupted by a homeless (one assumes)
Black man, wearing a disposable mask
but not maintaining a distance of One Alligator.

I shut the man's stories down
with my repeated "sorry's" (not worries)
and he went on his defeated, whatever way.

Sometimes, I'm appalling,
a filthy rag of a human being,
even though I'm a fanatical hand-washer.

More aptly:
Sorry, I suck.

We are all slow as molasses in January
(Dad's famous saying),
to learn
& relearn the most basic things.

11.10.20

"Thus it was I learned that Love was our Lord's meaning."

-Julian of Norwich

One Eye

The old man wears a face mask
and a white eye patch taped on—
marking an X—
so that his only feature is:

One Eye

I stare
at the man's unfortunate setup
(children and writers are allowed
to stare).

So many Job's walking around
on this weary earth, waiting for catastrophe
'round the next corner—a man can only take so much before
he breaks.

Last week,
Dad & Diane had to deal with
a flooded (carpeted) basement.

Yesterday, I heard about a local senior couple
whose home, which they had lived in for 40 years, had burnt
down.

The earth cries out—
The rocks, they cry out—

The old man's Eye notices my stare—
I look away, narrowly
missing a child
with ungodly light-up shoes.

12.23.20

Strokeaversary

Today marks 11 years
since my stroke
at age 32.*

Mom always spoils me
on this day.

This year, she sent me
a kitchen timer
& a beautiful notebook.

Soft, marbled mint green
& embossed in gold
are the words:

create & conquer

We learn a lot about our bodies
when they are stricken,
and we learn a lot about ourselves
in adversity. We surprise
ourselves. And we are surprised
by the love & care of others.

    1.   Human bodies are not a monolith.

    2.   Our fragile/sturdy bodies are incredibly smart and
        adaptable, the plasticity of our brains, remarkable.

    3.   Mom advocated for me like a Boss.
        She's always got my back, no matter what.

    4.   My immediate family, when they learned

I was in the hospital, rushed to my side, by air.

5. Aunt Kerry Jill sent me a beautiful,
    bright mustard prayer shawl,
    which warmed me,
    warms me
    with its healing properties.

6. Dad said I have **GRIT** (tattooed on my elbow & on my
    heart) (since covered up by a coffee plant).

11.10.20

*My stroke was caused by a blood clot, due to side effects from
birth control (estrogen). I'm living proof that messing with
hormones can be risky for a small % of people.

iPhone upgraded

Out of the Dust...

Out of an old quilt,
a flannel button-up,
a camouflage jacket, what have you,
my sister-in-law, Amanda,
makes the sweetest memory bears
w/signature leather noses,
for her customers.

As Amanda sews the fabric,
piecemeal, together,
she prays over each bear,
and the bear,
like Corduroy,
comes to life, in a sense,
bringing a bit of familiarity—
tangible, huggable—
to those missing,
aching for
their loved ones.

Held

10.22.20

Itch

I have the craziest,
most irritating, incessant itch
on my foot
that can't be eased
by scratching violently,
or repeatedly,
or not thinking about it,
or praying it away.

I itch
for us to move on,
to branch out—
internally
   & externally—
to accomplish
something.

We itch
as a people
for change, much needed change!!
And, then again,
for sameness,
a sense of *normalcy*.

We wish
for health to pervade
our bodies & our earth,
our cells & our soil,
for our communities to grow
wild, colorful gardens,
a rich bounty for everybody.

...

In August, a student's wife
hailing from Argentina,
knocked on our door
& presented us with a zucchini
as big as Bramwell's arm,
a pretty pattypan squash
& tomatoes, a wealth of tomatoes
harvested from the campus' community garden.

Carolina (masked) managed to withhold
her customary hugs & kisses.

...

Remember
to continue to (Orlando Jonathan Blanchard Copeland)
Bloom,
wheresoever you are planted.

(xox)

Seminary (Lat. *seminarium*): seed bed

10.23.20

"How strange that Nature does not knock, and yet does not intrude!"

-Emily Elizabeth Dickinson

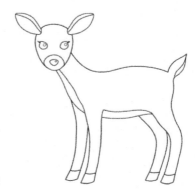

Pandemic Primer

Where life is involved,
things are always in flux, fluxing—
change is always in the air—
normalcy is an illusion,
sickness and death,
a hard reality.

Where faith is,
there is Life—abundant, yet
itching
for eternity—

Our magnet souls
housed in magnificent, not
indestructible
bodies of clay.

Waiting for,
longing for
Home—
God's house
has many rooms,
surely prepared for us
like Elsie Larson's guest room.

01.31.21

As the Weather Grows Fiercer and Colder

As the weather grows colder and fiercer
and the people migrate indoors,
among the bosom of family, friends & warmth,
a fire and poor ventilation,
COVID cases are alarmingly on the rise,
in the Midwest, and nationwide.

Sir Ranulph Twisleton-Wykeham-Fiennes,
explorer and writer, said:

"There is no such thing as bad weather,
only inappropriate clothing."

We're doomed.

...

Dining pods set up
outside of restaurants
are an innovative solution.

BYOB (Bring Your Own Blanket)

10.28.20

Church in the Parking Lot 2

Our poor Priest, dressed in ivory & a green knit cap
with a fat, gold pom-pom on top,
his robe blowing & billowing in the fiercest wind imaginable,
his heavy breaths heard over the low frequency radio,
his fingers freezing off, turning pages,
does his thing, reads the lessons like a fast-talking Gilmore
Girl, delivers the sermon,
doles out Hosts—hOsts flying out of the silver paten like
corn popping:

Jesus' flesh is carefully & dutifully picked up off of the
ground,
to consume, sans butter, later.

"The Gifts of God for the People of God."

(The People of God snugly in their vehicles,
sipping hot Coffee from travel mugs,
in the absence of Wine,
warm in your throat)

Holy Commitment.

...

"Please join us for Virtual Coffee Hour."

Zoom

11.01.20

Church in the Parking Lot 2:2

Following Church in the Parking Lot,
the Jr. Warden's busy & warm maroon SUV
with the NPR sticker in the back,
is declared dead—whilst the heater ran
& & the lights were left on.

Oh dear.

We watch from our cars,
mildly entertained,
as the Jr. Warden's maroon SUV
is surgically hooked up
to a willing parishioner's car
(new son-in-law scores points)
& & brought back to life in no time flat.

We press on, friends.

*

11.01.20

The Country is on the Edge of the Edge

Blessed are the Essential Workers

As the pandemic continues to infect
people left and right,
as people continue to shelter at home
or go to work & & work their butts off,
as mail-in votes are counted
& disputed
& recounted,

People are stressed *out*.
We're a nation totally freaked out.
Not to mention, heart-
broken.

Some children (adult or juvenile) have lost
both of their parents.

Some of our collective body, our members,
have died/are dying
alone.

Our nation, our world laments.
Our bent souls lament.

Screams from quarantined kids
next door
punctuate
the quiet.

11.04.20

It's Going to Be OK

Rachel Elizabeth Hollis, our Motivational Mother,
who has faced hardship and adversity with style,
moving her body all the while,
says that it's going to be OK.
We will handle whatever
comes our way.

"Take a breath. We got this."

"Swipe up to order my new book,
Didn't See That Coming."

Takeaway:

We are not in control.
We were never in control.
Focus on what is in your control:

Your lovely, imperfect self
& your actions, like making your bed,
like bringing an elderly neighbor flowers & cookies (if only I
had more time),
in the space of today.

11.04.20

Note: People in the public eye are going to make mistakes. And
keep making mistakes, because they're imperfect, fumbling
humans. This abrupt "cancel culture" is lacking in mercy, which
we all need, desperately.

"You get to decide what kind of attitude you're going to have when you have to do things that you don't want to do."

-Dad (Casey Affleck), *Light of My Life*

...

"Be kindly affectionate to one another with brotherly love, in honor giving preference to one another."

-Romans 12.10 (NKJV)

Prayer for a New Chapter: Help, Thanks, Wow*

Please keep Joe and Kamala safe,
under the shadow of your Wing,
as they work to help heal
our nation's soul
(a worthy goal).

Thank you for our First Dogs,
soon to roam the White House,
Major and Champ!!

Please help
the Donald,
both loved and reviled
and stubbornly stubborn.

Thank you for seeing the good
in each of us.

You have a covenant relationship
with each of us in your large, catholic family.

And for wishing your children to become
better, holier, steadier,
humbler people,
like our blessed Brown Jesus,
who oozes Love & offers his redeeming Blood to everyone.

Wow, our collective mood
is much improved!

Enough with the blasted fireworks already.

Amen.

11.07.20

*Nod to Anne Lamott, author of *Help, Thanks, Wow: The Three Essential Prayers*.

MY DOG IS A DEMOCRAT

Hope is Everything

The CT scan reveals:
R is cancer-free!

Although R is not out of the woods
yet re: his particularly nefarious
form of cancer
and he may never be,
he is held by a lavender
yarn-web of prayers.

While we are not out of the woods
yet re: Coronavirus & its stupid intent
on proliferating, proliferating, mutating, mutating,
Hope is here,
sitting with us
over peppermint, raspberry leaf tea
& Hope is coming, in the flesh, w/feathers,
to heal humans hurting, trees groaning, creation frowning
& & everything, everything.

In the thick of it and always,
Hope is our inheritance; Rejoice in hope!

R, his beard & & eyebrows slowly growing back,
celebrates with his beautiful family
over organic ice cream sandwiches.

:))

11.10.20

The Great Healer

Orlando Bloom adopted a rescue puppy ("a one year old something & something mix") named Buddy!

-@orlandobloom, Instagram, Nov. 10

As a young girl, I used to coax our Golden Lab, Buddy, who I called "Ol' Buddy Ol' Pal," to lick my cuts, believing that his tongue had healing properties.

I don't know how I knew this, I just knew it.

*

Of course now, in his lofty place with Jesus—
the Angels & Archangels taking turns taking him for long walks—Buddy's health & healing powers
are heightened.

(*wink*)

11.11.20

Confusing Times

Gus* looks at me with intense curiosity,
like: *What the hell is on your face*
(a mask) at least twice per shift (a mask) (meaning,
a persona) (and, literally, a mask).

Gus hardly ever leaves his condo,
favors watching Mass, old musicals,
instead of the news
and he is too polite to say anything.

I feel compassion
for seniors with dementia,
who are even *more confused*
during this perplexing crisis,
wherein confusion continues to be sewn.

...

11.14.20

*Name, etc. details, changed.

To-do

Today, I glued together
1 circular stone coaster
that has been broken for, like, 5 years.

Deep Bow

This time next year, I wonder:

Will we be setting our sturdy wooden table—
having placed the insert in the middle—
anxiously awaiting all of our healthy, happy guests?

...

We'll toast to health
& to each other.

clink

11.24.20

"The world breaks everyone and afterward many are strong at the broken places."

-Ernest Miller Hemingway, *A Farewell to Arms*

Church in the Time of Quarantine 2

In today's video update, our consistent Priest friend wears a clergy shirt & a clergy collar-round-the-neck.

At his right is a pool of bright light and a messy circle of bright light—halo-ish or corona-ish (*wink*) in appearance—sits precisely above his shiny head.

Interesting thing, light.

Photographers arrange their lives around it.

God is wrapped in it, light.

11.17.20

"...in Your light we see light."

-Psalm 36.9 (BSB)

Selfless

On Thanksgiving,
we receive a special delivery:

Our 2006 Toyota® Corolla,
damaged in an accident last winter,*
made all shiny & newish!!

Bryan Roy has worked on it
for months and months
(he knows where to find car parts
& how to haggle).

We're lucky to have
somebody who knows cars
in the family.

And, more importantly,
we're lucky to have
somebody who is kind & selfless
in the family.

Helper

11.26.20

*NOT my fault.

Grandma's Friends

Lavanche Lavonne,
retired Nurse, master Sewist,
beloved Grandmother,
still lives at home
in her cute, worn old farmhouse
with her bad cat, Sunny.

She has moved her bedroom
to the cozy living room.

Along the frosty windows
are set small, colorful vases
that reflect the light,
rainbow-like.

Grandma has more friends
than anyone I know.

Alone, Grandma
befriends the spiders
& the mice &

12.14.20

Grandpa Dwight

He liked bagpipes
and going for long hikes.

One winter season,
he went cross-country skiing
each & every snowy day (marked by an "X"
on the calendar).

He made wonderful food:
good, simple bread;
a variety of recipes utilizing his garden vegetables;
and Jeremiah's favorite: rice pudding.

As Dad carries Grandpa's name: Dwight,
so Jeremiah carries Dad's name: Jon,
and Beau carries his Grandpa's name: Jon.

Dwight Junior loved his dear wife, Lavanche;
together, they increased their love & light x5
and beyond, and beyond.

Grandpa delighted in nature's simple, bountiful things;
birds, wildflowers,
which he & Grandma pointed out & named,
so teaching their grandchildren.

How did we grandchildren get so darn lucky
in the grandparent department?

Grandpa had a great laugh,
sometimes uncontained—

And, sometimes he was sad.

12.14.20

Grandpa Bear

He was special to me
and I was special to him.

Dear Irene often reminded me.

As a girl growing up in a hard world,
Grandpa wanted to show me
the interesting, beautiful, sentimental
and historical parts of the city, of his world,
on a higher plane than mine.

...

When I was single and lonely
and I wouldn't give a guy,
any guy, seemingly, the time of day,
Grandpa Bear said that I had high standards.
And this quieted certain people.

...

Bramwell reminds me, a little,
of my wonderful and rare Grandpa Bear:
his intelligence, especially for history,
his care in making things special (for me, especially)
and his love for all things sentimental.

When Bramwell wears his soft, brown, suede coat,
I give him all of the bear hugs.

02.18.21

Note: written on Grandpa Bear's birthday. Grandpa had an affinity
for bears and he resembled, precisely, a friendly, grandfatherly
brown bear (minus the fur).

Rest

Recently, Grandma Priscilla Ann
has been moved
from her care facility
to her youngest daughter,
JulieAnne's, home.

Grandma lies in bed in the well-lit living room—
a homemade banner with hearts hangs above—
& Malcom, the little sable dog,
lies upon her.

Dogs, besides knowing things,
are our comforters,
living, breathing, heart-shaped heating pads
for our weary bodies.

Meanwhile, at Grandma's former facility,
there are 9 cases of Covid-19
(my family knows a worker on the inside).

...

Paper hearts in windows everywhere
one looks,
bear us up.

11.28.20

Priscilla (PJ), 92

My Grandmother, Priscilla,
always had a chic bob haircut*
and wore fashionable, well-made clothes
with a Nordic/German sensibility;
patterned wool sweaters, felt clogs.

She held her head high, a lady
and told funny stories
and looked intently at people
when they were talking.

Priscilla loved her beautiful daughters:
Kerry, Leslie, Wendy, Jody, Tracy, Julie.

I see Grandma in their noses & in their humor,
in their animated expressions,
in their chosen professions,
in the way in which they treasure family
and in their sentimentality.

Grandma's influences are celebrated
in Mom's funny stories
and in her way of making things;
food, birthdays, milestones,
so special for her kids (even
in the midst of struggle).

Priscilla's famous fudge cake—
the roof of fudge thick and rich,
set over a homemade white cake—
stands as *the* best cake

I've had the pleasure of savoring.

Also, not to be forgotten:

Grandma's Swedish meatballs, her hospitality
and the warmth, fun & tradition
of crowded (!!!) holiday gatherings:

Remember taking turns cramming together
on the couch in the sitting room,
for family pictures?

***

Grandma delighted in her grandchildren
& great-grandchildren, including
one darling girl who shares her name:
Clara Priscilla.

*

Grandma did not accept
one-armed hugs. She advocated
for real hugs.

Grandma's likeness is seen
in my comfortable
& unique fashion sense,
        in my body's shape,
in filling our home with hearts
& in my love for dogs.

Grandma *loved* her late dog, Mandy,

and her many other dogs & cats
& chattering birds,
enriching her one precious life,
through the years.

I seem to remember
Grandma keeping Muffin,
her late Calico cat awaiting
cremation, in her freezer.

Anyone share this strange memory?

...

In honor of my beautiful Grandmother,
Priscilla (PJ), our maternal matriarch,
friend and local acquaintance to many,
I drank a glass of sparkling rosé
& got a modern shag haircut.

P.S. It's OK to be sentimental
in writing about your Grandmother,
lover of the monogram.

*Let light perpetual shine
on Priscilla's head.
Amen.*

12/4/1927-12/1/2020

*Nod to Grandma's longtime,
skilled, gay, fun Hairdresser.

A Shot of Peace

She heard
the direct, merciful words:
Let her go
She felt a tingling
in her body, like it was being lifted up
She looked up
& felt & the & presence & of & Angels—
a spiritual presence
felt by everyone present in the room—

Say "Hi" to my babies,
Isaac, Jonah & Priscilla/Dwight
& to my Dad
& to Dwight

...

12.03.20

My hair has reached
Cousin Itt cult status.

It has become remarkably heavy.

Today, my Stylist (masked),
bravely about her business,
wearing a cute red French bob (I love, love, love bobs
but I don't have the right neck for them),
wielded her razor expertly
to give me (masked)
a modern shag.

I feel fresh & hip & new!

My jaw is currently un-
clenched
&
I'm levitating a little in shag land (not the British slang)

Lighter

now what do i do with bangs

12.05.20

Church in the Time of Quarantine 3

In today's video update, our consistent Priest friend, now bearded, wears a navy pullover with a snowflake pattern, over a clergy shirt & a clergy collar-round-the-neck.

He looks like he is on a holy ski vacation but he is in the church office with the out-of-sync audio.

On this day in 1955, Rosa Louise McCauley Parks was arrested for refusing to give up her seat at the front of the bus.

Soup container pickup is tomorrow from 9-11:30 a.m.

12.01.20

"I believe we are here on the planet Earth to live, grow up and do what we can to make this world a better place for all people to enjoy freedom."

-Rosa Parks

Holiday Cheer/less

People forcibly nesting
are busily decorating for Christmas
early this year.

Little Women pine garlands set above the fireplace,
cranberries & dried oranges hung about the tree,
*pretty white and/or rainbow lights craftily strung up inside
& outside of the home*

Thank you, good husbands, others,
for your hours of labor, per tradition,
each & every year.

...

Our plastic Ikea wreath
hangs on our door
all year round.

It's no fun
decorating with *somebody*
who, at turns, is reminiscent, sentimental,
grumpy & on edge,
whose X-mas memories are marked
by parents on edge.

Sometimes, parents
are poor models
of healthy relationships.

Each year, Santa left B's dad, Lloyd,

1 bottle of Crown Royal Canadian Whisky
in his stocking.

*

Fruitcake
(if you can imagine)
makes B's spirits
a little brighter.

*

Our Rector promotes
"good cheer & flexibility"
as keys to life and hard times

come again no more!

...

WE CAN DO HARD THINGS*
like have small Christmases.

12.03.20

*Nod to Glennon Doyle and her podcast.

Winter is Too Hard

When a certain sharp,
meaner than mean expression
your partner makes,
when he's frustrated
with you, his dear one,
his love (??),
makes you want to pack your bags
& & move to Arizona.

x

Winter is finally here
in Southern Wisconsin.

When I complain about the weather,
Wisconsinites like to remind me
that I live in Wisconsin.

x

I have always been very sure-footed,
like one wearing snow shoes and like a deer
in the snowscape,
except for that one time

I slipped and fell
& dropped my carrier carrying
3 almond milk iced lattés
& a new clay planter which broke
into a million & one pieces &

Out of character,
I cried like a baby; tears
froze to my face.

Hi, I'm a white girl
and I have problems.

...

On cold nights,
B always prays for those
who don't have
a warm bed.

12.12.20

Forgiveness/A New Dress

I spent all day
mad at my husband
and sick inside,
like I had swallowed
50 or so small cases
of waxworms.

I needed help
from Somebody higher,
more loving, clean and pure,
who knows me better than myself;
him better than himself.

Help

When I returned home from work,
my husband, the slammed door!
was fully penitent.

It's hard to stay mad at somebody
who is fully penitent.

In order to seal the forgiveness deal
sometimes, and to make softer,
I suggest that the Mr. buy me a new dress.

I have a closet full of dresses.

While therapy is a luxury,
retail therapy is satisfactory.

01.02.21

Evergreen

Nicholas Anthony is like our own Jimmy Fallon,
mixed with Ben Bailey,
mixed with a rugged,
God-fearing Wisconsinite.

He is the light of our family;
a White Spruce tree,
strung with colorful lights,
woven through his great brindled beard.

...

Nick is special: a Red-shouldered Hawk,
or a Whooping Crane,
a precious living thing that ought to be
protected.

Older sisters should stand up
for their baby brothers, too.

(Protecting not so much
their bodily structures,
as their spirits.

Or: defending both to the death!

12.21.20

Church marquees:

**A THRILL OF HOPE
THE WEARY WORLD REJOICES**

...

LET EARTH RECEIVE HER KING

...

**BE THE KIND OF PERSON
YOUR PET THINKS YOU ARE**

First Step

Margaret Keenan, 90, of the UK,
dressed in a polka dot jumper,

Is the 1st to receive
the Covid-19 vaccine.

My husband & I are currently
quarantined, awaiting

Results of our Covid tests.*

It is our 2nd test,
in so many months.

Pardon me, momentarily,
my tea kettle is screaming.

I chose the mug
with the red love heart.

Oscar turns his nose up
at dog biscuits.

He prefers Hobnobs
procured at World Market.

We love Her Majesty The Queen
(reportedly in good fettle)
& I'm bananas (buh-nah-nuhs) over Jamie Oliver.

12.08.20 →

*Not detected, respectively (false negatives??).

Notes:

On Dec. 29th, Margaret Keenan receives her 2nd jab.

Sandra Lindsay, a Nurse in Queens, NY, is the first U.S. citizen to receive the Covid-19 vaccine, on Dec. 14th (she received her 2nd dose on Jan. 4th, 2021).

In a *New York Times* article, Lindsay says:

"I feel like healing is coming. I hope this marks the beginning of the end of a very painful time in our history."

...

On Jan. 8th, 2021, Prince Harry & Meghan Markle announce that they will be stepping back as "senior" members of the royal family.

Perspective 2

Joni Eareckson Tada, 71,
fragile of body,
fragile of lung,
has been diagnosed
with the dreaded illness.

Joni, of course,
isn't worried.

She has placed all of her confidence
in the hands of Almighty God.

She dreams of
the hope of Heaven,
come alive.

When we shall see Jesus,
Face to face.

Here and now,
Joni chooses to focus her energy
on the vulnerable among us,
without the privileges
of top notch medical care; antibodies.

Friends who are isolated,
empty,
scared to death.

Friends who are deserving
of our protection,
love & respect.

12.22.20

Jeremiah Jon

My brother, Jeremiah ("Bullfrog"),
handsome, athletic,
competitive and good at everything,
learned today
that he has Covid-19.

Jere, Type A personality,
also has Type 1 Diabetes.

He says he feels like
when he had Mono,
many moons ago.

Yesterday, his lungs were clear.
Today, his cough has grown worse.

A few days back,
Mom brought Jere a meal
and sat with him.

We are a praying family.

I know in my soul
that Jere's going to be OK—
brought up out of the muck
& set upon a rock,

Even tho his texts
are brief & have a
positive bent.

12.19.20

Walk-thru Communion on Christmas Eve

There is our Priest!
In our church!
Double-masked, bearded & jovial,
dressed in white (more of an eggnog).

Our church is decorated simply
with 2 (silk but who can tell) poinsettias,
joyfully in their places on the altar
& a real Christmas tree.

Stained glass windows are propped open
but the church, she is yet cozy,
peaceful, prayed over,
a place prepared for us in the mess.

Our Priest says a service
for the Reception of Holy Communion
under Special Circumstances.

My husband & I hold out our palms, like panhandlers
& they are, as expected,
filled with the Bread of the Strong.*

Masks on.
Full hearts.
Can't lose.

We Exit on the left
and we are brought to a table full
of lovely, homemade Christmas cookies,

almost—if I squint my eyes & click my heels 3x—like at Grandma's house.

12.24.20

*Nod to Saint Maria Faustina Kowalska, *Divine Mercy in My Soul: Diary of Saint Maria Faustina Kowalska*.

Oh Owl

At the curve in the road, driving home
in the dark of Sunday night,
we come upon what looks to be
a Mackerel tabby cat or a
big marble cake?

But no: It is a majestic Owl
with unblinking fearsome yellow eyes.

The Owl is upright, unmoving
but for its freaky rotating head
and giant knowing eyes.

There is nothing to be done
but be on our way,
our headlights on bright.

I wonder what Jeremiah,
who works summers for the DNR,
would have done.*

12.27.20

*He may have moved the Owl off of the road. Jere says that
sometimes, owls don't wish to leave their prey. Like moms don't
wish to leave their sick babies (always babies) alone (without
Mom).

Only Daughter/Journal Therapy #3

Our Oscar,
still full of energy & *joie de vivre*, like Dave Hollis,
but declining
as dogs do, as people do,
now whines
to be let up on the bed,
the chair.

He is down to a handful of foods
that he can stomach
(he loves turkey & grazes
his senior dog formula).

Sometimes O is unsettled
& he wants to go out, repeatedly,
during the night,
for no discernable reason—
he is wearing us *out*
in his old age.

& I won't go into detail concerning
his increased "accidents"
on our beige (gross, I know) carpet.

Poor old boy,
whose snoring has grown
louder (& cuter).

Speaking of snoring, when B
(his snores could wake the dead)
was a child,

his family gave a home
to a young Schnauzer, Cindy,
to pep up their old Schnauzer, Fritz.

Bramwell, who says that we are strictly
a 1-dog family, resembles a Schnauzer
in the head.

That said, we have an agreement (in writing)
that if I get cancer, I get to have
a big dog (a Standard Poodle like Scott E. Jordan).

...

Our Bichon Poodle, Oscar,
is like a baby gorilla, a black sheep
& a glorious Afro,
rolled into one.

He quite relishes
being the one & only dog.

...

Sometime after the boys came along,
it was all over
for the only daughter and
the Dad.

If the only daughter shared
the interests (hunting, fishing, sports)
of the boys and their Dad,
she would be included

but the only daughter
liked Art
and being alone.

They say I'm spoiled.
But I had/have to be compensated somehow!!

P.S. My bros. made life fun,
which is the most important thing (*wink*).

01.01.21

My favorite pic of Nick and I (Credit: Jody Lee)

Mom is a Raw Nerve Housed in a Rind

Mom is a raw nerve
housed in a rind.

A life of hard knocks,
of lemon rinds & hard work,
is hard for one soft body
to bear (although she wears it well).

Now retired, Mom
keeps busy with projects,
decorating, framing
the rust.

I want always to be
the raw honey (if not the money)
in her tired, dusty life.

...

She dreams of
her family living & working together,
in a communal hive,
closer.

She dreams of
a small house to keep,
with a few animals,
not including cows:

Chickens, a dog.

A window to look out,
whilst hand-washing the dishes.

She finds peace
sitting by the water.

01.25.21

Mom and Jeremiah (Credit: Jody Lee)

Mom is a Raw Nerve: Addendum

Each daughter walks the plank
to the Dentist's chair,
where she will have teeth drilled and pulled and filled
without Novocain (or laughing gas or other nerve blockers).

Their mother did what she could,
raising 6 girls, having allergies, of a kind, on her own.

Another mother takes on a 2nd job,
so that her daughter can have braces.

01.25.21

Scribble

I have just discovered Margaret Eleanor Atwood's poetry.
My husband (Canadians are proud of their stars)
gave me *Dearly* for Christmas.*

Atwood is in another league, a whole separate strata of Poet
and Writer,
set apart:

She is a happy witch from outer space
(Toronto, actually).

If we had money,
we'd move to Toronto in a heartbeat.

If we had money,
I'd enroll in Art school, pronto.

A favorite Writer (and mostly disappeared Author),
Haven Kimmel, as I remember, decided not to
be a Musician,
because she knew she'd never be great.

Some things you have to do,
because you have to do them,
middling or dribbling or great.

For the love of God, Mike and Pete,
Go & do your thing, fumbling, bumbling human friend!

12.25.20

*Purchased at our local bookstore. Read "Blizzard."

Be You

In a video update posted by our consistent Priest friend, he talks about a book he read on the Apollo astronauts. When one Astronaut was asked how he or other astronauts were changed after their mission, he said that everybody came back more themselves.

After this crisis passes, will I be more of who I am?

Will you be more of who you are, beautiful?

...

04.01.21

"Be who you are and be that well."

-Saint Frances de Sales

*

"I love people being the maximum version of their character. I love people being themselves."

-Kanye Omari West, *My Next Guest Needs No Introduction by David Letterman*

Sometimes, Time Heals

Ten years ago, I took a poetry class in a Detroit suburb
taught by a gritty, good poet who said that you have to eat,
sleep, breathe poetry if you want to be a good poet
(likewise, good chefs say this about reading all of the
cookbooks and tasting & eating all of the food, and elite
athletes train like nothing else matters).

Anyways, the poet, a hip, white guy w/stubble who ran on
black coffee, ripped one of my little poems—a poor gazelle
in a cloud of smoke—to shreds, so wounding my little
anima.

In hindsight, the poem needed *work* and I was pretty naive
about Black women and their struggles, which meaning,
along with others, the poem tried to carry.

But there's healthy criticism, and there's eviscerating a
poem, a person. I was accustomed to mostly gracious
commentary from peers.

...

Some people, wounded of soul, never return to church, or
they return & & have panic attacks when worship music
plays.

Some other people, when it is time (healing, like poetry and
like growing a beard or a plant, can't be rushed), and when
they have sufficiently mended, bravely
decide to give church,
give poetry another chance

& they fall in love, again.
...

Joy Harjo returned to making music
after she was 40.

Joy Harjo's poetry will make you cry—in a good & healing
way, in a way that stirs you to mend & work to mend.

This is how we grow
rich:
by honoring each other.

03.09.21

Church People Ain't Perfect

When church people and personnel—
people in positions of higher power—
disappoint, inevitably, on a small or large scale,
it's magnified, because of their representational
positions, because we look up to them
in our humble positions.

One church member with free will
can, 1. Write them off, break up the band,
or, 2. Forgive them, of the Church, of their infraction/s (as
you see things, feel things, anyways),
because they are humans, doing their best (we pray),
in their appointed and/or anointed positions.

When so many heightened, hard-edged, heart feelings
(it's hard to argue with your feelings) are involved,
forgiveness—no longer resenting but embracing (figuratively
and/or literally: when you have both been fully
vaccinated)—
doesn't come easy, man, woman, friend, foe.

But we, sheep, are tough of soul—
with the Holy Spirit as our Captain (individual & collective)—
to forgive, because we have been forgiven
so many times we have totally
lost count (our somersaulting souls turned
upside down & inside out).

Forgive often

04.18.21

Opinion Pieces

Your opinion is:

-Seemingly leaning, like the classic V8® commercial.

-A fish swimming opposite its Episcopal school of fish.

-Suspect, like Joan of Arc's visions of light.

-A person held in solitary confinement, unfairly, lonely.

-A person with a brain injury who can't speak, only write,
    obsessively.

-A Mennonite woman wearing a plunging V-neck, chopping
    onions.

-Hippy-dippy: Go hug a tree and while you're at it, a lightning
    bolt.

-Individualistic, egotistic, you're a statistic.

-Possibly mistaken: One may have more to learn because one
    doesn't know everything, or even half of everything.

-Out there: in the wide world, in your lonely, self-published,
    or traditionally-published book.

-Your truth—proceeding from your unique experiences, your
    worldview, your body, your soul.

-Above all, a puzzle piece valuable to the whole (hold your
    head high).

04.04.21

Jeremiah is OK

Although Jere, sturdy and well made,
didn't know if he would ever
again be OK.

He couldn't stop coughing
& his headache was ever-present
& his body ached
& at night, he "slept,"
splayed on the bathroom tile—
only arising to vomit or dry-heave (gross).

He wanted nothing more than to sleep
but he couldn't find sleep
like new mothers,
insomniacs or
fugitives.

Oh Jere.

Jere says that his better half
never gets sick.

Or, he says, maybe she's a carrier—

Today, Jeremiah took his fun-loving son, Beau (Jeremiah Jr.),
ice fishing (Perch were caught).

Mom can breathe, again.

...

Mask-makers and I
hold different definitions
of the word "breathable."

12.28.20

162

Happy New Year!

Bramwell began *War & Peace*,
while I'm trying to finish an overdue
graphic novel.

It'll be nice, sometime this year, hopefully (isn't hope
the worst),
to have our libraries back,
with their cast of local weirdos,
super friendly staff—
including the transgender person
who became themself, wore fuchsia lipstick,
right before the public's eye—
Gracie, the therapy dog
& even wild kids, wildlings &
getting their germy germs all over the place—

We're all wild works in progress—

01.01.21

Note: B finished *War & Peace* on Jan. 29th.

CAN'T WE ALL JUST GET OOLONG?

WTF is Happening

The fire alarm inspector arrives in the a.m.
and your poor dog hides under your desk
for the rest of the afternoon
jumpy & & barky

...

A pro-Trump mob storms the Capitol!!

Forcing House & Senate members—
steadily working to certify & swear-in
,, sweaty hands resting on the Bible—

Joe Biden as President
, Kamala Harris as VP—
to shelter under their desks
w/safety hoods

...

Mike, his pet fly & Nancy are spirited away—

...

It is all Appalling

An embarrassing stain
on our collective carpet (made in China)

Chinese kids, hands down, are the cutest kids on the planet.

01.06.21

Easy

I didn't even need to offer so much as
an explanation
to be let in
to the secure apartment building,
per usual.

I look trusting. And I dress like a child,
w/style.

Men from WI, especially, are easy.

*

It takes elderly persons *ages*
to buzz me in.

What?

12.04.20

Good Deed for the Day

Our Corolla was good and stuck—
gridlocked, as it were—
having made deep grooves
in the snow and ice.

Oscar and I panicked for a minute
just before a strapping WI guy
in a Green Bay Packers hat,
with a pom-pom on top,
put his good-natured Pit Bull
in his black Ford F-250,
and pushed our car
out in 3 tries.

I honked "Thank-you!"
to the Good Wisconsin Samaritan.

He waved,
acted like it was NBD,
let his BFF out for a walk
on the groomed trails.

01.07.21

Little Loretta

Mom wondered if her dear little granddaughter
would remember her...

Little Loretta ran to her like a soft magnet with arms
open wide,
waved good-bye to her parental units,
for but a short time.

...

Loretta Kay doesn't know me.

We are both missing out

On love & family & fun & (healthyish) snacks...

I sent Loretta (reportedly, already interested in shoes)
(girl after my own heart)
a pair of little hot pink Crocs®
to match my camouflage Crocs®
worn with hot pink socks.

01.12.21

January Blues

We're all just exhausted,
wary, dusty, crusty,
not at all peachy.

Our Corolla is no longer
safe: Exhaust is creeping in
to the cab.

If ever there is a time
for a Crying Heart tattoo...

Or, a Sacred Heart tattoo,
or praying hands
holding a rosary
& hand sanitizer.

Sorry, Mom.

Mom, who is ultra-careful
in the way of germs & such—a germophobe,
one could say—
plans to visit
on my birthday:
Something to look forward to.

01.15.21

Holding Each Other Up Like Easel Backs

She looked forward to our visits,
so that she could see her son—her prized one—
and have a bath:

I would help her out of her deep tub
& hand her a big, fluffy purple towel—
she could manage the rest,
in her pretty peach bathroom
at the top of the stairs.

Going slowly down the carpeted steps,
my mother-in-law stopped to take the double-hinged
frame of her and her beloved son,
into her well-cared-for hands
& press a button:

Trevor (Bramwell) had recorded
a sweet message for his mum,
telling her that he loved her,
which love she accepted exclusive
of all others (since the passing
of her beloved husband, Lloyd David).

Once, Jackie Marion took me aside
to tell me that when she goes,
Trevor will *fall apart*.
She was right.
We did our best to hold him,
bowing low to the earth, upright.

R.I.P. Jackie (who would be just *horrified* to see her name in print)

01.17.21

Cancer, Again

Phone calls are not welcome (same).

Cards are welcome.

No words suffice.

Although, I've learned
that the right words, soothing words
are expected,
from those who call
themselves writers.

Right words are expected
from Priests, Pastors, Deacons and Rabbis,
whose job it is
to say the right thing
(impromptu or litany)
and/or to listen.

Pray in earnest, people of light.

May the Daughter of God,
our talented, skilled friend,
have complete healing
of throat and body.

Amen (so be it).

02.28.21

Simplicity

In 2006, I spent a month
at our cabin in the woods,
mostly reading, journaling
and, at night, watching movies
(video cassette tapes!), borrowed
from the tiny, rural public library.

In the spirit of simplicity,
I brought my French press
and ate the same thing every day
(protein bar; salami sandwich; rice & beans),
including one good book per day,
anointed w/olive oil.

I could *maybe* text
if I climbed the precarious stairs to the loft
and stood on the bed with my hand raised
in the rarified air—

One night, lying in bed,
a mouse scampered
across my body:
I almost died.

For protection from backwoods rapists,
I slept with a hatchet
under the mattress.

...

Some smart people

have created
specific boundaries—
some involving lock boxes—
to keep their respective phones
unglued
to their respective persons.

And some people
have sworn off it, social media,
for the sake of their wondrous souls.

...

You're permitted to just be,

To focus your pretty little head
on the real richness
of life, for a season,
or for always.

See how it feels,
weigh it like freshwater
in your hands:

simplicity over algorithms

*

Serious writers
don't listen to a lot of music,
watch a lot of movies,
to free up more space
in their days

and in their set apart
heads & hearts.

And they, most real writers,
and my Dad,
could care less
about social media
(unless forced w/an electric cattle prod
by their publishers).

...

How do you want to be
at age 43,
23 or 93?

I want to be ALL IN,
like God is ALL IN,
moving towards my best self.

But how can I bid farewell
to my Instagram "friends"?

01.01.21

Not Today, Satan

Inauguration Day

Fraught,
we, the people,
the wounded people, wait

For the babe to draw
her first breath

For the sacred oath
to be bestowed

For the holy hand to be placed
on Joseph Robinette Biden's bent head,
on Kamala Devi Harris' raised head
(not on Kanye's head) (we still love you, Ye),

The blessing of democracy.

*Your words are astoundingly good,
hopeful & beautiful, as are you
& your amazing fashion choices,
Amanda S. C. Gorman.*

A new day.

JESU MERCI

01.20.21

Can We Talk About Lady Gaga's Inauguration Outfit

OMG, it's perfect.

Wild but not too, yet very Gaga: Grand, Glam &
Awe-inspiring/eye-catching-&-pOpping...

Her giant flowing (floating) red silk faille skirt:
A grossly large & beautiful rose in bloom—a rose bomb—
Sudden blood underwater, rising to the surface,
A trail of smoky red elegance...

A simple fitted navy/naval jacket pinned with a giant gold
Dove—wings outstretched—an olive leaf in her beak,
At the lady's beating heart, signifying:

Life, Hope, Freedom,
Peace on earth, Goodwill toward women & men

Her suffragette white leather gloves are also a nice touch.

A bold red lip, crown braid—braided thru
          with a black ribbon—
And 2 red poppies in back,
          tying the look together:

Princess Leia x Frida Kahlo x the Queen of Hearts*

You nailed it,
Lady Gaga & fashion house,
Schiaparelli!

01.20.21

*But a force for good, rather than evil.

44

Mom will be 64 this year.
Bramwell will be 54.

In their presences,
I am only (mostly) myself.

May I strive to ever be only myself:

Crunchy peanut butter & raw, local honey
On Brownberry whole wheat (crusts intact).

Like Bernie Sanders
& & his homemade mittens.

Amen.

01.24.21

Mothers are Soft Warriors

My young mother,
after I was born early,
trekked up a great hill,
crossing a great river,
3x daily
for 2 weeks,
to nurse me,
her little buttery miracle.

This whilst working on packing
for an imminent move
to the Twin Cities

& trying not to tear out
her stitches.

***

We do what we must,
like noble mothers:

Malleable warriors
wearing gold breastplates
forged into
sun lamps
formed into
glittery gold stars

Halos above our
cherished
miraculous

globular
bright new heads

***

01.24.21

BORN TO BE MILD

"In peace I will lie down and sleep,
for you alone, Lord,
make me dwell in safety."

-Psalm 4.8 (NIV)

...

Shadow
Shadow

Mr. Groundhog
saw his mythical shadow,
of course,
witnessed virtually—
because the world has gone virtual—
of course.

More waiting,
more winter,
more staying in.

Did I mention more waiting?

For spring
bloom
warmth
birdsong
open windows:
light, life,
Hosta eyes poking out of the brown, fertile ground—

02.02.21

"Groundhog Day also shows us that the monotony ends.
The cycle will be broken."

-A member of Punxsutawney Phil's "inner circle," cbsnews.com

My Mask is Better than Your Mask

Walking the halls
in the all quiet senior apartment building,
we (masked), going slow as turtles and following the rules,
pass a well-dressed older man,
who holds a black leather glove loosely over his mouth,
looking pretty guilty,
like O.J.

Tsk tsk

Meanwhile, snarky, swiftly-
moving middle-aged women at Target
double-mask.

masks-on-masks

The earth is littered w/disposable masks
& tampons
& & plastic everything that eventually-never degrades.

& asterisks,
if you look close.

*

02.09.21

Wednesday Praise

Snow is melting,
snow-women & men
with tripart shapely bodies
are melting,
icicles are falling.

Oscar Poscar, our furball,
burrows in the snow
with the utmost Glee!

Like a playful river otter
& a lamb hop-hopping about.

***

While much less energetic,
Grandma, home alone,
is doing well.

A few weeks ago,
she slipped on the ice & fell,
hitting her poor head
but she is OK:
nothing concerning,
no broken bones.

The sun shines bright
on our Wednesday,
the clouds look like soft cotton batting
in the vast wide open sky blue sky

02.03.21

Love and Life

"a miserable bundle of imperfections"

-Saint Maria Faustina Kowalska

It's nice to have somebody
on your side,
who loves you
and likes you—
with all of your miserableness,
dryness,
sinful illness
& & innumerable particularities.

And egoism.
And extreme introversion (I'm the husband who only likes
being around one person: his wife).

I could go on about his attributes, like:
He patiently answers my questions all day long
& he is the perfect husband 83% of the time.

And his bad, unbecoming spots, like:
He has the emotional makeup of Spock
& a child with colic.

...

For Valentine's Day,
I gifted him Dove® chocolate hearts,
a Star Trek mug
& a 12-volt window defroster.

He gifted me a lilac spring dress,
printed w/tiny cornflower blue flowers,
exchanged for a lilac romper,
exchanged for a gray-blue sweatshirt with ruffles
at the shoulders
(fitting for the round-shouldered woman,
wholly incapable of holding
a purse
strap).

02.14.21

Quotation: Notebook 1, *Diary of Saint Maria Faustina Kowalska*

Dental Thought Engine

Half my lower lip is numb,
gums, cheek,
tooth roots, whatever,
half my lingual frenulum, too.

When Jeremiah was young,
his lingual frenulum had to be snipped—
he could then lift his tongue
& curl it into a roll of bologna
which Mom didn't often buy,
as it was thought to cause cancer,
like everything.

When one is left alone,
at the bottom of a cistern and
marooned in the dental chair,
there is a lot of thinking to be done...

When Jere was in surgery to free his tongue,
he choked on his mucus (gross)
and needed to be intubated—
obviously, Jeremiah was OK,
lived to torment his big sister
another day (JK).

...

Around this time, our poor cat, Inky,
after chewing on an electrical cord,
lost half her rough li'l tongue,
which, by the way, grew back.

All is not lost:

A recurring theme of scripture
and of life.

It's *impossible* to keep my tongue, tongue, tongue, tongue,
tongue still
when stressful, invasive things
are happening in my mouth, you?

Why can we command our tongues
in some ways, but not in others?

...

Once, out to dinner with family—
were Mom and Dad still tied together, then?—
Jere, staring at my two front teeth,
said that it looked like little men
were dancing a jig
on my teeth,
which image I, too, saw,
regrettably (so initiating a lifetime of
self-conscious, toothless smiles).

...

My beautiful American Indian Dentist—
wearing five coats of mascara—
is humming,
to calm me,
while she maintains a death grip
on my rightmost jawbone.

02.16.21

Oh Brother

When I was in high school
& & I had surgery to remove my wisdom teeth,
so weakening in wisdom (*wink*),
one side of my face swelled up unbecomingly:

Nick said it looked like
I had a Jumbo Jawbreaker
in my mouth.

My brothers are unfortunately good at similes.

Following the surgery, Mom stood waiting
with a large strawberry malt,
an Angel of Comfort

02.16.21

Note: B received his 2nd dose of the Pfizer vaccine today; his arm
swelled up a bit. An older woman I know reports "brain fog,"
weeks after getting the vaccine.

Dear Jeremiah

May God grant you forgiveness
for the childish act of hurling
a wooden bat up onto the roof
of our 2-story lake house,
in an unconcerted effort to get down
the sturdy, country-blue square pillow,
which we co-opted for 2nd base (sorry, Mom)
& the bat's unfortunate trajectory—
working in tandem w/the Law of Gravity—
to make contact w/my precious head,
made higher by my position
standing atop the cable reel drum,
whilst putting serious *thought*
into just how to get the
dang pillow, pillows, down.

Amen.

But, really, I forgive you.
No lasting harm was done
(that I know of).

And I'll stop mentioning this
unfortunate incident,
every time I see you
and your ~~unfortunately~~ amazingly strong arm, arms.

Hugs (you still owe me $5),

Jos

Crowned

My heightened dental anxiety,
on top of other anxieties of the day,
was alleviated, somewhat,
by a soft pink blanket
warm neck pillow
shades drawn
lights dimmed
music muted
a mini water bottle
a 5-min. break when my mouth
was too tired
& & much
unwarranted praise.

I could get used to this royal treatment.

...

1 ceramic crown prosthetic
feels weird: a hard, gummy puzzle piece
with mountains &
          & valleys,
smooth grooves & hollows.

Sensitivity on chewing.

We have *a lot* of *The Crown*
to catch up on.

Mom is crowned[4].

02.16.21

Walking Styles

Husband: "Now that you have a crown,
do I have to walk two paces behind you?"

Wife: "You already do."

Bramwell walks,
at all times and in all places,
like he's meditating
in a labyrinth;
I, on the other hand, walk fast.

When crossing the street,
but not in winter, or when I'm carrying grande iced lattés,
we hold hands automatically:
our hands soft, supple, automatic magnets.

**

While Trevor Bramwell Richards has a tattoo
of an eternal Trinity symbol
on his left forearm,

Harry Edward Styles has a tattoo
of the Holy Bible
on his beautiful left forearm
(a cover up).

02.18.21

If I Only Had a Brain

Moms hold an understood grace
for intellectual failings,
like temporarily forgetting their children
's names,
or forgetting their respective Frappuccinos (oops)
on the roofs of their respective SUVs:

Mom Brain

Now I, too, have an excuse
for forgetting common words like "cattails,"
or leaving a burner on,
or forgetting to wear a bra:

Pandemic Brain*

02.18.21

*"Pandemic brain" is the general feeling of overwhelm,
depression, fogginess, etc., that some people experience during
this prolonged pandemic.

"Covid brain" is used to describe the symptom/s that some
people report during Covid and post-Covid, characterized by
lingering confusion, headaches and short-term memory loss.

Ashes

A cross
on my
forehead
+
specks
of ashes
(burnt palms)
on my face,
like old mascara,
fallen from
defined lashes
or
course
ground
pepper

...

I'm ashy,
sooty, dusty,
dirty,
decaying

The lot of us
but dust

Forgive us
rascally,
abashed
people.

Amen.

02.17.21

Proud to be Oneida

Rest in Peace, Lee "Gordy" McLester III,
Machinist, Veteran, Author and Editor of many books
On the history and culture of the Oneida Nation—
      so preserving the oral tradition—
Member of the Oneida Hymn Singers,
Married 60 years to Betty,
Proud Father, Grandfather, Great-grandfather,

Recipient of an eagle feather.

We belong to the yawning earth,
And to our great and glorious, knowing Creator.

Lee, 80, died of Covid on May 26, 2020.

May your rest be this day in peace,
And your dwelling place in the Paradise of God.

02.23.21

-Book of Common Prayer 1979

Winter Weather in Texas

An unexpected, vexing development,
wreaking havoc on
people and pipes,
vehicles and green sea turtles.

When the struggle was *already* real.
People were *already* maxed out.

But people pulled together, with moxie and grit,
housing and feeding each other,
delivering sea turtles to warming stations,
being Good Texas Samaritans.

Our own kind Texans,
here at our woodsy Wisconsin seminary,
often found spaced around the fire-pit—
a remedy for the malady of separateness—
are in dire need of
winter dressing (if not driving) lessons.

(Yes, I'm aware that I dress like it's winter
all year round—I run cold.)

02.28.21

194

On Giving Up Social Media for Lent

One may, at long last, recognize—
after a reckoning of worthwhile
and not so worthwhile—
a feeling of saturation,
of overwhelm,
of needing to press
pause.

...

Miraculously (or not so miraculously),
I have more time
to read, or to stare at the boring doings of ladybugs,
or to do or don't do whatever I fancy.

Life doesn't feel so rushed—like I'm always
running out of minutes,
of day.

I feel calmer, more
open
present
more receptive to people
& to the Holy Spirit,
freer, truly.

A friend, when she gave up the 'Gram
a few years back,
felt like she got her *soul* back.

*

Anyways,
In my smallest sacrifice,
I have found a better way, hey.

Selah

02.21.21

Confession: Fast broken on 03.15.21, when I was sick as a dog
(not with Covid) and snapped at my poor husband to leave me
alone. I will begin again, tomorrow. Fast broken again when I had
my period, and yet again—I'm entirely hopeless (not really!).

Church in the Parking Lot 3

It is a beautiful day.
The parking lot is filled and spaced,
appropriately.

Our church sits on a popular lake
where ice fisherpeople, arising early,
attend ice fishing church.

Our Priest is in fine fettle,
wearing a pea coat,
black Keens
and double-masks,
over his great, brindled beard.

I sip my lemon ginger tea
& & ask my husband questions,
during the speedy liturgy.

It is somewhat well
with our souls,
anchored, as they are, by hope.

But people and Priests
in the MKE diocese
are restless
for a safe return to semi-regularity,
for enlarged borders,
expanded life,
further fishing prospects...

03.07.21

Helen's Roses are Wilting

Helen's roses are wilting,
crumply,
darkened,
but they, with baby's breath,
stay in water,
stay in the vase

Which is unlike her

Helen's cancer has returned;
from her breast
to her bones

She is a spreading tree,
a Willow—her roots tough,
her leaves finely-feathered—
one who delights in the sun

water, woman, life

Helen is thankful for her family,
for comfort food, gnocchi,
for a mug of ginger (real ginger) tea
and for her abundantly peaceful home,
with its many wide windows

While Helen understands more
than most,
she doesn't understand
how some love God
like a father, husband, wife, brother, friend,
but she will

03.04.21

Toothache

Tension headaches
and dull aches
where I had my crown placed,
keep me up at night, keep me
fairly miserable throughout the day.

A young woman I know
said that every member of her family
is currently suffering.

Our dog is sick
after indulging in something totally gross
(that is, delicious).

The sun is hiding out today.

Asian Americans hide out
in their homes (due to ugly racism
and hatred: detestable hate crimes).

We love you, Sandra Miju Oh (Asian-Canadian-American),
and we're so sorry.

...

Deep breath in—
and out—

I have my mug of Bulletproof coffee
with brain octane oil & ghee
& half an hour to write,

before work
with my beautiful,
terminally sick client,
who reminds me that life
is terminal.

Everybody has an expiry date:
We are all finite
as night.

Our hearts ache
for rest like flowers ache
for spring.*

Maybe the sun'll come out
tomorrow, tomorrow...

03.10.21

*Nod to Rupi Kaur, author of *Milk & Honey*.

Note: March 11th, 2021, marks the 1-year anniversary of the Covid-19 shutdown. There has been 500,000+ deaths from Covid in America. Worldwide, 2.8 million people have died from the virus.

Hear My Humble Cry/Contents of My Shoulder Bag

In these hard, uncertain, chaotic, historic times,
my cries for help have become protracted to include:

Angels, trees, saints, Mother Mary,
characters in books I especially identify with—

These beings, of course, in addition to:

Jesus, my constant helper in all things, at all times
and bosom friend to the end.

I keep a well-loved,
red comfort cross,
a gift from Mom
(*squeeze*),
in the zipper pocket
of my shoulder bag, also
housing my notebook,
2 Zebra ballpoint pens (fine pt., black),
my name badge & lanyard,
a menstrual cup & Ibuprofen (for emergencies),
a Gin-Gin (ginger not gin),
a sm. bottle of gin (for emergencies),
a pack of Kleenex
& & & 3 thumb drives.

03.18.21

Things are Finally Looking Up

We're all so freaking tired of these dark days gathering dust
But, things are finally looking up:

What with vacations—I mean, *vaccinations*—happening,
Vacations and vaccinations happening,
Churches & public libraries safely reopening
        (among those already open),
Hi-tech air filters filtering,
A 2nd round of stimulus checks arriving,
Spring slowly arriving,
First flowers blooming among
        the damp, fallen leaves,
                abandoned masks
        & remaining deposits of unclean snow.

We all wish for the damn pandemic
To be behind us (we're so over it), for the world to open up
And say "Ahhh":

Help us to press on toward the prize—
Are we there yet? Are we there yet? Are we there yet?
Has the car stopped moving?—
Hold on a little longer, walk on
        in the hallowed, earthen mystery of Shadow &
Light—

03.16.21

"How long, O Lord?"

-Psalm 13.1 (ESV)

Palm Sunday People (Episcopal Edition)

Windy and cold in Wisconsin,
we church people are all bundled up,
fitted with good-fitting masks,
ready to walk inside our pretty lonely church,
excited to welcome her people like a Grandmother,
red doors propped Open:

One parishioner, a Teacher, Photographer
and Card-maker, wears a red mask
with li'l white hearts,
which totally sums her up: All Heart.

An older woman with a white bob
doesn't recognize me,
disguised in a knitted burgundy hat & matching mask.

I don't recognize the above older woman
without her less able-bodied,
sweet sister (God rest her soul) & walker;
the sisters were a matching Memory® pair,
making their way to the 3rd pew on the left.

On the altar,
green palms stand erect on either side
of the covered, carved Cross,
the oxblood-shrouded Cross
like a red kite
about to take flight
from this heavy, crazy earth—

...

Following the dispersal of palms,
the Junior Warden automatically hands off
the palm in her palm
to the lovely parishioner missed at the far left;
the JW swiftly takes a palm
that had fallen to the red-carpeted floor
w/the low pile.

I'm pretty sure
a tall pile of bejeweled crowns awaits
the Jr. Warden, loyal wife & fun mother,
who knows where all the good consignment shops are at.

Today, I went with a heavy brow,
pink highlighter like war paint
& my gray-blue sweatshirt with ruffles at the shoulders;
soft, wrinkled wings.

The Rector's kids, Red and Yellow, Black and White
(especially loved by our congregation), sit with friends,
listening attentively to their father's 5,000[th] sermon.

A large old man, hunched over
& wearing buffalo plaid,
sits in the front left pew (the Gospel side),
matching our Rector at the pulpit,
in oxblood chasuble & black stripes.

Dad's uniform is buffalo plaid & brown Carhartt pants.
I miss the old man.

On the way out,
the old man nods to me (I exiting from the Epistle side)

w/a twinkle in his eye (if you look close),
like a Grandfather who has found God;
I return his nod.

The Rector, in his short sermon
(due to the looong Gospel reading),
holds a microphone like a 70's talk show host
(reportedly, the wireless mics
gave up the Ghost).

Lutheran church bells chime
not on cue, not on cue, not on cue,
during the good sermon.

A child at the back is fussy
(remove him at once!).

I write in my notebook:

"Love moves over
          & makes room
& makes space
for others to be."

Our Organist, made lovely and whole (*whew*),
reunited with her donated organ (*wink*),
sings of the foal of a donkey
& the Daughter of Zion:

Her voice is somehow clarion
whilst wearing a mask (how can it be?).

My Deacon sits reverently in the quire

(minus the choir),
wearing black cassock,
under white surplice
w/oxblood stole, modified

(He also wears the crew socks
with a folded hands motif,
I set out for him this morning).

We lay down
our coats & our sweaty palms,
our ideas of how Victory!
should be won, overrun by Love.

"Walk in love, as Christ loved us
        & gave himself up for us,
a fragrant offering
& sacrifice to God."

03.28.21

-Ephesians 5.2 (ESV)

Thursday of Mysteries

Yellow nautical rope
has been replaced with
wide red wine ribbons,
sectioning off pews.

The Rector wears
his eggnog chasuble
with the wide red stripes—
long lines in front & back—
black Birks.

No foot-washing
will be done
this evening.

No incense
will be censed.

On the altar,
1 candle stands
on either side of the
Cross, center stage.

...

Following the Sacrament,
the Rector moves the elements
from their marked places
to the sacristy.

He wipes down, with care,

207

a kitchen table after supper,
the bare wood altar
and "kisses" it.

It is silent.

We wait.

...

Back at the seminary,
students sign up
to keep watch
in the Red Chapel.

B will keep watch—
his Smartwatch set—
from 3-4:00 a.m.
whilst Oscar & I
get our beauty rest.

(Our apologies, Jesus.)

...

04.01.21

Empty Cross

Gold Cross
Shrouded in black
Translucent silk
Light—diffuse—shines thru

Sometimes, the dark—contrast—
Is beautiful

Gothic,
Heavy,
Somber cobweb

Silence
Beheld
On the sacred stage

Echo of
Christ

04.02.21

Note: written whilst watching the Washington National
Cathedral's Good Friday service on YouTube.

Easter Sunday: Eyes Wide Open

I'm woken by birds chirping LOUDLY:

He is risen!
He is risen!!
He is risen indeed!!!

I ditch my Easter frock
for a soft pastel flannel
& pink Vans® slip-ons.

On the way to church, I pass
three gleaming white SUV's, in succession.

Listening to Keith Green's "Easter Song,"
I pass the long lineup at the Dunkin' Donuts drive-thru
(Good news: God loves cocaine & sugar addicts, alike!).

...

On the church steps,
the Rector's mature daughter,
who has developed a cool, gothic style,
reminiscent of my teenage self (two words: **black eyeliner**),
carries a water bottle with a prominent sticker:

ANTI-RACIST

Our fashionable Usher
wears a peacock-feathered headpiece, leads me to
my sectioned-off pew,
where parishioners wave to each other

from their prominently marked worship spaces
& sides.

Our radiant Organist wears a bright purple
headpiece; a giant, festive bow
or "nest" atop her head,
as one stylish Brown child said.

On the altar, carefully decorated by our Rector,
we see big white blooming bells, or ears;
pink & white popcorn balls sit
in the colorful stained glass window above;
plus more donations of blooming bells & & joyful yellow
blooms bursting forth below—

Stained glass windows are propped open allowing in
loud bird song, Lutheran church bells &
& motoring fisherpeople, etcetera—Everybody's welcome,
here.

I count *15 candles*, including
two sets of three oil candles on the altar
& the tall, waxy Paschal candle—Light overcoming darkness
all day long—positively glowing.

In the ornate, embroidered design
of the cream pulpit fall,
I make out a silly Rabbit,
her delineated green ears to hear Raised & & Alert.

The bell sounds—

We, the people—

pressed, heart-broken,
hopeful & ready—Stand:

Alleluia, Christ is risen.
The Lord is risen indeed, Alleluia.

***

04.04.21

The Opening Acclamation, The Holy Eucharist: Rite Two,
BCP 1979, p. 355

Dogwoods in Blooming Bloom

You're terribly pretty, aren't you,
With your giant white/rosy/pink show-offy blooms.

But, um, your floral fragrance
Is *way too* "in your face."

Like some seniors whose
Sense of smell (among other witherings) has, too,
        diminished, faded like the green grass:

They are slow-walking perfume & & cologne ads,
Leaving suffocating trails of artificial scents in their wakes—

(Proof positive that in some instances, masks are not
The Worst Possible Things in the World.)

04.12.21

Untitled

Oscar is fading
and it's the saddest thing in the world.

I mean, I know it's not
but it feels like our whole world is diminishing
by the minute
and we never saw it coming
quite this fast,
all of his bright energy
suddenly stalled, stilled—
he stands around staring at me
(I mean, I know I'm interesting...)

Can he manage one more trip
to the dog park?

...

Oh Oscar,
our great love & joy,

Our joint-best friend
(his joints arthritic, his teeth in bad shape,
who knows what other sinister processes
are going on in his minute body)
& friend to all,

Except for that Maintenance dude
in our Detroit apartment building,
whose pant leg he
wouldn't let go of—

We don't want to let go
of our good boy—

I honestly thought that my fierce love
sustained him
(or at least the olive oil
I added to his food, served to sustain him—

04.09.21

R.I.P. Prince Philip, Duke of Edinburgh, 99

"He has, quite simply, been my strength and stay all these
years..."

-The Queen of her husband, Prince Philip, in a speech on their
Golden Wedding Anniversary, 1997

Love personified

Mara

The little girl with dirty pink Crocs®
& a little distressed jean skirt
walked along the sidewalk, just
ahead of us, naming things.

How old was this tiny human,
smarter than she should be?

Something about her cute face
struck me as not quite right;
a little doughy,
a little spacey,
her too-sparkly eyes weren't quite right.

Is she alright?

Is she *real*?

The little girl pointed to her house
& a voice that I couldn't place—
feminine/masculine/other?—
told her, Mara, to come inside, *now*.

Mara kept walking.
The voice kept calling.

Suddenly, I heard steps behind us
& a man who looked exactly like
a Native American Gollum w/long brown hair,
picked the girl up;
the girl cried out—

She only wanted to keep walking
in the cool of the day,
alongside my cute little dog & I,
he running a little slower these days.

Yesterday, on the 2nd Sunday of Easter,
Bramwell added Oscar to Prayers of the People.

...

I do realize that I don't know anything
and that kids need reasonable discipline,
but I wanted to keep walking with Mara.

I wanted to pluck all of the (imagined or real) bitterness
out of her life,
and keep her safe
and happy as a clam,
in our little womb.

04.12.21

Empty Well

I emptied
Oscar's water dish
& a tidal wave
hit me,
knocked me to
the vinyl tile,
where, earlier today,
Oscar lay
beside his water dish.

In Oscar's absence,
our little house
is an empty well.

An empty well which
we are working to fill
with our tears.

04.13.21

R.I.P. Oscar

(Oscar's diagnosis: splenic mass that had ruptured, leaving his
belly full of blood.)

"Everything's the same as when Golly was here. It looks the same...it smells the same...but there's this tiny hole inside me that wasn't there before."

-Harriet M. Welsch, *Harriet the Spy* (1996 movie)

Untitled Shadow

All of our rituals
and routines
are missing

My hiking
reading
being
companion
is absent—elsewhere
wagging

My perpetual shadow
is gone

For the first time
in 10 years,
I am alone

grief is grief is grief

& ugly-crying is OK

Be gentle with yourself,
you who have lost

Be gentle, careful with
your partner, too

Hold each other;
your furrowed brows,
your contorted, grotesque faces
& & your sad hearts, up.

04.15.21

"Death is always near us, walking beside each of us as a constant companion."

-Pastor Mark (Mark Crumpton), *Faith's Song*

...

"The Lord is near to the broken-hearted
and will save those whose spirits are crushed."

-Psalm 34.18, "The Psalter," BCP

An Outpouring of Love

A neighbor writes
an "Ode to Oscar,"
calling him a "holy hound"
and making mention of his
"soft and wise eyes."

Another neighbor knocks,
bringing us a sweet sympathy card,
a tiny succulent in a cute bunny planter
and homemade, chocolate-filled
bao buns, which smell heavenly.

Many cards have been
received, with thoughtful words,
including cards from our Veterinarian
and our Priest.

Aunt Wendy & Uncle Ken text us
a wonderfully empathetic video,
offering up a sensitive prayer.

Thank you for reminding us
that we are not alone
in our heavy emptiness.

How long will this heavy emptiness
last (an estimate)?

Black mothers, others, are also dying
to know.

04.16.21

I Prefer Blank Sympathy Cards

Pro tip (listen up, Jere):

When you (finally) phone someone who is suffering, who has lost, don't:

1. Say the things that you are supposed to say, and 2. Be the first one to end the conversation, hang up, because you're turkey hunting.

P.S. I know that I'm making much over grieving our dog, when others have lost human family members and friends, jobs, homes and more. I'm sorry if I, irked, seem insensitive. Grief—whatever the circumstance or form—makes one insular (for the introvert, even more so). Niceties go out the window, rightly so.

> It's me, myself & I,
> my raw meat grief
> & my perpetual stomachache &

> ...

P.P.S. At least you reached out—unlike *some people*.

P.P.P.S. Sorry that I never reached out to you, Jere, when your good hunting dog, Champ, died, when you found him one sad morning in his crate, his body hard as a rock.

04.17.21

The White Button

We are told to take as much time as we need.
Which are very comforting words, in themselves.

We are here to say good-bye
to our good boy,
whom we have had with us
for most of our marriage,
for a decade.

We will stay here in this little room
with light-filtering shades drawn,
with our good boy,
mouth clamped shut (B tries
to persuade O to lick him one last time, to no avail),
Oscar swaddled in a plush blue blanket,
looking weary, still (all of his vast energy
expended, expanding all around us...
still full of love and concern (his big brown eyes
the most beautiful thing in the world)
for his people,
for the rest of our days.

We are told to press the white button
whenever we are ready

I say all of the things I need to say
(my voice calm and loving, like a mother's,
which surprises me);
B says all of the things he needs to say via
tears
heart

tears
soul
tears
tears
t
e
a
r
s

...

Miraculously and practically,
we arrive at a place
of readiness and peace
(not panic).

In less than a minute,
our good boy
is at rest.

...

In a little while,
we will receive
Oscar's individual ashes
& a clay paw print.

...

Oscar never got to run & play in his fenced-in backyard that I
dreamed for him.

04.18.21

Untitled (quiet)

A mama bird
returns to her nest:

Empty of eggs,
of offspring

...

Our house
is so quiet
(just the way I like it)
but an empty-quiet

Not that our doggie was loud, persay—
except when defending his people
and/or his territory: his *presence*
was the thing that filled our space

Perhaps, if I may, it is a bit like the belly
of a miscarried baby—
womby white noise,
eternal emptiness
at the end of the anemic rainbow

...

Perhaps it is like the Holy Spirit
uninvited to the party of a soul—
waiting in the silent wings of forever
to swoop in,
or, No way, José

...

Sometimes I hear (I *think* I hear)
the jingling of
Oscar's thin aluminum ID tag

Like the jingling of bells at
the Eucharist

The jingling of bells in
another dimension:

Heaven, perhaps

...

04.20.21

Odball dog, you were ours.

Sweet-toothed (you loved ice cream) & salt-toothed; ever-licking your smitten master.

Curled up like a cat, or open to the world, on your back, you slept.

Adventurous, always up for an adventure, your strong back legs trembling w/the thrill of life!

Running home to me, long lost love at sea, is my best dream.

Oscar's Ashes

It is a beautiful day: sunny blue skies, breezy,
Cirrus clouds looking spiritual;
it seems right. Here
seems right.

Bramwell has printed off copies
of a prayer by Rabbi Barry H. Block, that we will take turns
reading, our voices breaking.

Before entering the gates of the dog park,
sans dog, sadly,
and making our way to the bench
under the Ash tree,
on which we often stopped to sit
for a minute,
we have a picnic (I choose a turkey sub,
in Oscar's honor)
(Oscar took bits of turkey so gently—was this learned
behavior, or innate to his wonderful, gem-like being?).

...

Bramwell carefully unwraps
Oscar's ashes, wrapped in wine-colored tissue paper,
revealing a plastic bag partially filled w/packed dust,
which dust we study:

The ashes are light gray, fine,
more like soft, pulverized sand, than ashes,
which ashes leave a chalky residue
on my hands
which I do not wipe away, which residue of life
I shall never wipe away for as long as I live.

As we disperse the ashes to the wind,
to the grass, daisies, tall weeds, trees,
ashes fall onto us;
onto our arms, legs, sandals,
into our mouths, ears, nostrils, open
souls.

We are quiet.
We take pictures on our iPhones (populated with pics of
Oscar).

We sit quietly, remembering
our good dog, dogs
coming up to us, wishing only to love & be loved;
one ginger-colored Poodle-mix appropriately named Jinger
wriggles between
our legs & onward—

A Jack Russell terrier barks sharply at us like something is
definitely off; his shaggy owner ushers him onward & away—

As we exit through the gates,
sans dog, sadly,
a woman asks, "Did you forget your dog?"

I tell her, briefly, about our Oscar
and she expresses her sincere condolences,
they on their 8th dog.

"May Oscar's memory bless our lives
with love and caring forever. Amen."

...

ACKNOWLEDGMENTS

Thank you to my Canadian husband and personal Deacon, Bramwell, provider of coffee, potato chips, love and books, during this pandemic. And to Mom, my #1 fan, always offering up prayers like (fragrance-free) incense, always looking to bless.

Thank you to the wonderful writers, Mary Oliver, May Sarton and Laurel Lee, whose poems, and journals, respectively, have provided solace and joy.

Thank you to Dawn, a wonderful friend and Poet who wrote the most kind Foreword, who sends her friends beautiful, handmade cards (we have saved all of them).

Thank you to Helen, avid reader, who has been a steady voice of reason during this hard time. I have especially enjoyed our rides through the park, watching the trees change.

Thank you to Aunt Wendy, Diane, Mary M and Steph, women who are great encouragers, which is everything.

Lastly (but not leastly), thanks for reading, dear Reader! While I'm a beginner poet, I think it's important to bravely put yourself and your hard work out there—in whatever stage of growth you're currently in—for anyone who will listen. Also, while my hardest year+ may not look like your hardest year+, this was simply my experience.

Love & much hope,

Josie

Don't lose heart,   *beautiful people!*

Contact me:

email: josielrichards@gmail.com
facebook.com/josielynnrichards

xox

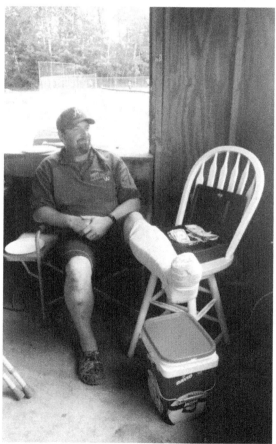

Jeremiah Jon (Credit: Jody Lee)

&

Made in the USA
Monee, IL
29 July 2021